BEIJING STREET VOICES

About the Author

David S.G. Goodman is a Lecturer in the Department of Politics, University of Newcastle upon Tyne. He was formerly a Research Fellow at the Contemporary China Institute, London School of Oriental & African Studies, and was educated at the universities of Manchester, London, and Beijing (Peking). His previous publications include *China: The Politics of Public Security* (1976), with the late Tom Bowden; *A Research Guide to Chinese Provincial and Regional Newspapers* (1976); and various articles on Chinese politics and society in the academic press. He spent the academic year 1978/9 in Beijing.

BEIJING STREET VOICES

The Poetry and Politics of China's Democracy Movement

DAVID S.G. GOODMAN

MARION BOYARS
LONDON · BOSTON

First published in Great Britain and the United States in 1981
by Marion Boyars Publishers Ltd
18 Brewer Street, London W1R 4AS
and Marion Boyars Publishers Inc
99 Main Street, Salem, New Hampshire 03079

Australian and New Zealand distribution by Thomas C. Lothian
4-12 Tattersalls Lane, Melbourne, Victoria 3000

British Library Cataloguing in Publication Data

Goodman, David S G
   Beijing street voices.
   1. Political posters, Chinese
   2. China – Politics and government – 1976 –
  I. Title
   301.16'1   JQ1516   79–56846
   ISBN 0-7145-2703-3

Library of Congress Catalog Card Number 79-56846

Photoset by Specialised Offset Services Limited, Liverpool
and printed by Robert MacLehose & Co. Ltd., Renfrew, Scotland.

CONTENTS

Appendices

List of Illustrations of Chinese Poems and Photographs

This book uses the standard Pinyin system of translations from
Chinese throughout. Thus, for example, Peking appears as Beijing.

LIST OF POEMS

THE SONG OF LIFE IN MY SOUL

Friends, do you love life?
If you do,
The hard road must be your constant companion

Friends, do you know life?
If you do,
Struggle must be your pleasure in life.

朋友，你爱生活吗？

如果你爱！

艰辛就是生活的伴侣。

朋友，你知道生活吗？

如果你知道！

奋斗就是生活的乐趣。

《生活》编辑部

Editorial Poem of *Live* No. 1, p. 10.

BEIJING STREET VOICES

Woodcut from Jintian 1

PREFACE

The aim of this book is to present an anthology of poetry from Beijing's Democracy Movement during the winter of 1978/9, and in doing so to sketch the development of the movement from November 1978 to April 1979. China's other voices are rarely heard in the West, and China's other poets still more rarely. However, the first five months, from the Democracy Movement's emergence in late November 1978 to the regime's first real attempt at a clampdown in late March, early April 1979, have provided plenty of opportunities to find, read and hear uncensored poetry – the Beijing Street Voices of the title. Not that all the poetry presented here is 'great' poetry by anybody's standard. On the contrary, it is very much poetry of the moment, and selection has been biased towards providing a representative sample of the poetry, politics and publications of Beijing's Democracy Movement. Thus at least one poem has been selected from each of the major publications to appear during those five months.

The poems selected for inclusion in this volume are all taken from the unofficial publications of the Democracy Movement in Beijing during November 1978 to May 1979, and have been translated by Lynda Bell, Susette Cooke, Ian Honeysett, Christina Jansen, Ian Lea, Alistair McBain, Jana Verunačová and myself. In translating from the Chinese, an attempt has been made to translate each poem as a poem – to capture both the emotional and literal levels of meaning, if and when necessary, when and where possible. As a result some of the poems have been quite freely translated. Rhyme and meter in Chinese (which are far more common than in English and essential features of traditional poetry) have not always been reproduced in the English version. On the other hand, rhyme or meter have sometimes been added or adapted to produce an English equivalent of the Chinese. Thus, for example, the satirical epithets of 'Animal Crackers' (p. 21) which contain no rhyme or meter in Chinese, have been reproduced in

English as rhymelets.

Explanatory notes to each poem have been added where necessary, and both the poems and the Democracy Movement are set in their social and political contexts. In addition, a selection of documents from the Democracy Movement which are not readily available elsewhere are included. They are the initial publication statements and editorial comments of some of the unofficial journals, and an analysis of the Democracy Movement by one of its activists. Not included are those documents which have been published elsewhere. By far the two most important not included are the '19 Point Chinese Declaration of Human Rights', which can be found in *Index on Censorship* September/October 1979 (Oxford University Press, London); and Wei Jingsheng's 'The Fifth Modernization – Democracy' which can be found in *Documents on Communist Affairs, 1980* (Macmillan, London). Finally, this volume also includes a Glossary of Chinese names, terms and places, and a checklist of all the unofficial publications known to have been produced in Beijing from November 1978 to 4th May 1979.

Obviously, much of this work has been a collective effort on the part of the translators, and I would like to thank them all for their enthusiasm, cooperation, encouragement and trust. In addition, I would like to thank all those in Beijing and Newcastle for their invaluable help and assistance, not just with the creation of this book but also more generally during my stay in China. In particular I would like to acknowledge my friends and teachers at the Beijing Language Institute and Beijing University, Department of Economics, where I spent the academic year 1978/79; Nigel Wade of the Daily Telegraph for his interest, friendliness, and the photograph of myself in Tiananmen Square on 5th April, Annemarie Rule for her, as ever, extraordinary secretarial skills; J.J.G. Hanratty, who ensured that this project was completed; and last, but by no means least, Felix, who first suggested the idea and whose support has been invaluable. None the less, I should stress that, the poems and quoted passages apart, I alone am responsible for the ideas and opinions expressed in this book.

This book was finished by December 1979. Obviously, neither China nor the world have stood still. The Democracy Movement and its activities, as described here, have disappeared for the time being, perhaps forever. The political context of many of the poems and much of the Democracy Movement's activities changed in many ways after the Spring of 1979. Of greatest importance, there has been the rehabilitation of Liu Shaoqi. However, none of the changes has invalidated this essentially contemporary account of the Democracy Movement. For that reason, I have decided not to update the few references to the wider political context, but to leave such references in the time frame in which they first occurred.

David S.G. Goodman
University of Newcastle-upon-Tyne.

CHAPTER ONE

Introduction: Democracy, Protest and Poetry

首钢工人李铁华在演讲。

罗小韵摄

Tiananmen Square, 5th April 1976

THE DEMOCRACY MOVEMENT

In the second half of November 1978 a new, and to a certain extent popular, movement erupted on the streets of Beijing. This was the self-styled 'Democracy Movement' which soon spread to other cities in China and has caught the imagination of some in the West as a 'Human Rights Movement'.[1] In Beijing alone during the following months there were mass-meetings in Tiananmen Square in the heart of the city; demonstrations along Beijing's major thoroughfare, Changan Jie (The Avenue of Eternal Peace) and in front of Zhongnanhai, the headquarters of both the Chinese Communist Party and the Government; and a partially successful attempt to establish a free speech area – at first named 'Hyde Park' – to the west of the city centre in front of what is now known as 'Democracy Wall'. There was a veritable epidemic of wall-posters not only on Democracy Wall but also on walls and buildings along the city's main streets, and even on the People's Republic equivalent of advertising billboards – the huge red signboards more often than not bearing quotations from Mao Zedong which stand at almost every major crossroad. Finally, and a particular characteristic of the Democracy Movement, there was the flourishing of an unofficial press. Throughout the winter, usually on Sundays at or about three o'clock in the afternoon, crowds gathered at Democracy Wall to buy the various magazines, newspapers and pamphlets produced by individuals and groups specifically for that purpose.

To describe all these activities as being part of a 'movement' is to a certain extent to imply a greater degree of uniformity in ideas and unity of organization than actually existed during the period covered here – namely, from mid-November 1978 to the first major attempt by the Beijing authorities to bring the Democracy Movement's activists to heel at the end of March and beginning of April 1979. Organizationally, there was no single Democracy Movement. Rather, there were individual activists and groups which had been formed either as self-styled 'mass societies', such as the China Human Rights Alliance (*Zhongguo renquan tongmeng*) and the Enlightenment Society (*Qimeng she*), or around the publication of the various unofficial magazines and journals. On occasion, some of these groups may have come together to issue joint statements or hold meetings. For example, on 25th January 1979, the Human Rights Alliance and the Enlightenment Society together with the 'April 5th Forum' (*Siwu Luntan*), 'Exploration' (*Tansuo*), 'Masses' Reference News' (*Qunzhong cankao xiaoxi*), 'The People's Forum' (*Renmin luntan*), and 'Today' (*Jintian*) – all of which are or were 'mass newspapers and journals' – issued a joint statement in a wall-poster on Democracy Wall, which pledged them all '... to persevere in carrying out the long-term struggle to realize socialist democracy ...', and a policy of mutual support in defence of their constitutional rights.[2] However, cooperation was not always the order of the day. There was often conflict in the Democracy Movement, not so much between the various groups (although this too did occur) as within them. Thus, for example, both the Enlightenment Society and the Human Rights Alliance split at the end of February, beginning of March, for both political and personal reasons. The former split into three, two parts of which kept the same original name, while the third was newly established as 'Thaw' (*Jiedong*). The Human Rights Alliance merely split in two. However, both parts continued to use the same names for their organizations and publications and each claimed to be *the* Human Rights Alliance.[3] For the most part then, the Democracy Movement existed more abstractedly in the minds of activists as a social movement in which they were participating.

Moreover, the lack of higher level organization and unity is not surprising when one considers the wide range of perspectives brought to bear on China's past, present, and future, as well as life in general, and expressed through the Democracy Movement. Attacks on Mao Zedong, opposition to the Chinese Communist Party (CCP), and demands for human rights were undoubtedly the most sensational aspects of the Democracy Movement, particularly for the Western observer, but they are far from telling the whole story. Arguably the most radical, but certainly the most clearly articulated analysis was that of Wei Jingsheng in his 'The Fifth Modernization – Democracy', first produced in two parts in two wall-posters on 5th and 20th December 1978, and later published together in the first issue of 'Exploration'.[4] From a self-stated socialist standpoint, Wei criticized Mao and the totalitarian system he and his 'small group of sycophants' had created. For example, when considering the Chinese economy's previous setbacks, Wei described them as:

> ... disasters caused by the autocratic rulers, by Fascism under a Marxist-Leninist signboard, by totalitarianism, and by those who toyed with hundreds of millions of human lives according to the vagaries of a small number of persons.[5]

In its place Wei advocated freedom, democracy and human rights. Indeed he argued that without such conditions the government's policy of the 'Four Modernizations' was unobtainable.

Catching up and surpassing Western levels of economic development and technology had been part of the Maoist vision since at least the mid-1950s. In 1964, at the first session of the 4th National People's Congress, Zhou Enlai had first proposed the modernization of industry, agriculture, science and technology, and national defence – the 'Four Modernizations' – to Western standards by the end of the century. As a slogan it was ignored during the Great Proletarian Cultural Revolution, but was later resurrected in 1975.[6] Since 1976, the achievement of the "Four Modernizations" has been a guiding principle of national policy.

In contrast, although the Human Rights Alliance produced a 'Nineteen point Chinese Declaration of Human Rights'[7] it did not attack the Communist party state and contained only a passing swipe at Mao's deification in its first point. On the contrary, the Declaration was couched in quasi-legal language, and sought the guarantee of human rights both within the constitution and by the intervention of the state.

Attitudes towards Mao Zedong varied from the head-on opposition of Wei Jingsheng to the hagiography of the anonymous poster writer who, in a wall-poster dated 30th November (1978) on Democracy Wall, not only called for support for Mao and carried his picture, but also praised him as 'a modern Lenin' and predicted that his detractors would soon be suitably punished. In between these two extremes, there were various shades of opinion. As one anonymous railway worker wrote in a wall-poster of 22nd November 1978

> We recognize that Chairman Mao was a great Leader of the Chinese people, a great figure in China's history. However mentioning his achievements does not mean that he made no mistakes.

That particular wall-poster like many others held Mao responsible for the errors of the 'Gang of Four' during the last two years of his life, suggesting that they could not have acted as they did (especially against Deng Xiaoping in April 1976) without Mao's support. Others, such as that appearing on Democracy Wall on 24th December 1978 and signed by 'A Young Woman', accused Mao of having inflicted ten years of civil war and suffering on China by launching the Great Proletarian Cultural Revolution in 1966. This too, was a popular attitude as reflected in wall-posters and the unofficial press. Indeed this was the line taken by the very first wall poster to mention Mao directly by name on 19th November 1978. The writer was not totally anti-Mao, and praised him as a 'great leader who led the nation to many victories' and 'creator of our Marxist-Leninist Party and State', however, the poster writer continued:

> From 1966 to 1976, China was under a fascist regime and the only persons who defended us ordinary people against the fascists was Zhou Enlai.[8]

Similarly, attitudes towards the CCP and the state varied

from degrees of hostility to degrees of support. Nor were such generalized discussions and debates about the roles of Mao and the CCP, or the need for human rights, the only subjects dealt with through the Democracy Movement's activities. There were repeated calls for the 'reversal of verdicts' on those of Mao's opponents during the Great Proletarian Cultural Revolution (GPCR) or even before, who had been publicly criticized, humiliated and removed from office in disgrace. These included demands for the rehabilitation not only of Peng Zhen,[9] the former Mayor of Beijing and the GPCR's first major victim, but also Liu Shaoqi,[10] the 'Number One Person in authority taking the Capitalist Road' of the Cultural Revolution. Almost anything could, and was capable of exposure through the Democracy Movement from the specific to the general. Thus, for example, unpopular leaders such as Wu De (the Mayor of Beijing until late October 1978), Wang Dongxing and Cheng Xilian, all three of whom were and are Politburo members were repeatedly criticized;[11] individuals with real or imagined grievances they wished to see redressed could give their causes wider publicity; and particularly as the Democracy Movement developed other general issues such as sexual freedom, wage reform, economic and social differentials, privilege, and international relations were given an airing.

Unsurprisingly, 'Democracy' had different meanings for different people, and in many ways merely replaced 'Revolution' – predominant during the decade of the Cultural Revolution from 1966 to 1976 – as the shibboleth in the new language of politics. According to one commentator in the unofficial press, it implied the immediate 'withering away' of party control in basic-level organizations.[12] Others conceived of it as Liberal Democracy, Capitalism or Christianity, and even, as in one case, all three together.[13] Both the United States[14] and Yugoslavia[15] were suggested as models of democracy for emulation. Wei Jingsheng defined it in terms of maximum individual freedom and non-Marxist socialism in 'The Fifth Modernization – Democracy'. One somewhat surprising (given its association with the 'Gang of Four' during the GPCR) definition that was suggested was the Paris Commune.[16] However, for the most part any future democracy was conceived of as being under the leadership of the CCP, even though at times this might entail some amazing contradictions.

Moreover, right from the start there have been two major aspects, or rather emphases, to the Democracy Movement – one more political, the other more cultural. On the one hand, there have been those, such as the publishers of 'Exploration', the 'April 5th Forum', and 'The Spring of Peking' (*Beijing zhi chun*),[17] and the Human Rights Alliance for example, who have concentrated on problems of political democracy, and if not actual involvement then at least the reportage of current affairs. On the other hand, there have been those whose primary focus has been what can be called 'Cultural Democracy' – that is the attempt to free art and literature from the restrictions in style and content imposed by the official media, and in so doing to provide alternative media of expression. Perhaps the most popular of those has been the group surrounding the publication of 'Today', who have not only produced that literary magazine, but also organized poetry readings and various art exhibitions. Others have also produced literary magazines, for example 'Fertile Land' (*Wo tu*), 'Harvest' (*Quishi*), and 'Live' (*Shenguo*), and indeed as the political legitimacy of the Democracy Movement was increasingly questioned by the CCP after January 1979, there was an observable tendency for unofficial publications, particularly new ones, to stress that they were literary magazines, thereby attempting to imply that they were non-political.[18] However, the emphasis on either politics or culture has been just that and the two kinds of activity have not been mutually exclusive. Thus two of the aims of the 'April 5th Study Group' (*Siwu xuehui*), which later became and produced the 'April 5th Forum', one of the leading 'political' journals, were:

> ...To publish the people's thoughts and words, which for all kinds of reasons are not contained in official publications. To publish popular literature which develops the spirit of April 5th ...[19]

On the other side, 'Today' in an editorial 'To the reader' in its first issue pointed out the need to 'go a step further in deepening people's understanding of the spirit of freedom'.[20] Moreover there can be little doubt about the political nature of many of its contributions, as for example in the Swift-like 'Animal Crackers' which ends this introduction, or the dry cynicism of 'A Story of Fish',[21] taken from 'Today' numbers one and three respectively.

For all these reasons then the Democracy Movement is best defined by its activities rather than by its content, except at a very generalized level. Common to all those activities was the theme of greater freedom. Most sensational were the demands for political democracy, but from a wider perspective there were the equally as important (and possibly more effective) requests for cultural democracy. More narrowly, there were demands for individualized freedoms and the redressal of personal grievances by those who themselves felt, or on behalf of those whom others felt, had been victimized by the Cultural Revolution and 'the system'. It would be an exaggeration to claim that all tendencies were represented within the Democracy Movement, but the range of opinions was wide and there was no single idea of the future proposed, no agreed meaning to the concept of 'Democracy.'

On the other hand, there was agreement about the Democracy Movement as a reaction to the now officially declared 'tyranny' of 1966-76 and a vehicle for both debate and self-expression. For the activists – be they writers of wall-posters, producers of an unofficial magazine or newspaper, or poets who read their works in public – the Democracy Movement represented the right to have options, to discuss opinions, to experiment, and to self-expression, even though they differed as to the limits they sought to place on such activities. Nowhere is this aspect of the Democracy Movement shown more clearly than in the publication of 'Science, Democracy, and Law' (*Kexue minzhu fazhi*). Produced roughly once every ten days by students from the China Traditional Opera College, 'Science Democracy, and Law' is a digest of all the wall-posters which appeared on Democracy Wall.

Unlike the other unofficial publications of the Democracy Movement it was not sold, but passed from hand to hand and posted on walls and buildings around Beijing in order to ensure, and inform, a wider audience.

Elsewhere, the Human Rights Alliance when discussing the Beijing Party Committee's reaction to the Democracy Movement in late January 1979, in its publication 'China's Human Rights' (*Zhongguo renquan*), defended the right (as they saw it) not just to be either for or against Mao retrospectively, but also to attempt an assessment of his strengths and weaknesses.[22] Poster writers not only answered previous wall-posters but welcomed the disagreements and consequent arguments in the spirit of 'Otherwise why have a Democracy Wall?'[23] Finally, 'Today', in its first editorial, saw the events of late 1978 as the antidote to '"The Gang of Four's" cultural despotism':

> Now our generation can sing the song that's been in our hearts for ten long years ... Today, as people open their eyes anew, we should never again take such a narrow view of 9,000 years of cultural heritage, but start to use a broader perspective to survey the surrounding horizons. Only in this way can we really discover our own value, and thereby avoid ridiculous conceit or deplorable self-defeat.[24]

Moreover, the right to have differing points of view and to self-expression were re-inforced, not only in 'Today' but also in almost every unofficial publication, by reference to:

> Comrade Mao Zedong's policy of 'Let a hundred flowers bloom, a hundred schools of thought contend'.[25]

This policy, now commonly known as the 'two hundreds', was first announced as the CCP's post-1949 attitude towards intellectual activities in May 1956. At that time it was interpreted as:

> ... freedom of independent thinking, of debate, of creative work; freedom to criticize and freedom to express, maintain and reserve one's opinions on questions of art, literature or scientific research.

although such freedoms were not extended to 'counter-revolutionaries'.[26] The following year, in a speech to the enlarged Supreme State Conference of 27th February – 'On the correct handling of contradictions among the people' – Mao spoke at some length about the slogan of the 'two hundreds'. For Mao the slogan meant that:

> Different forms and styles in art should develop freely and different schools in science should contend freely. We think that it is harmful to the growth of art and science if administrative measures are used to impose one particular style of art or school of thought and to ban another. Questions of right and wrong in the arts and sciences should be settled through free discussion in artistic and scientific circles and through practical work in these fields.[27]

Although the slogan became unadulterated cant during 1966-1976 – apart from anything else administrative measures were used to impose one particular style of art and to ban others[28] – it has been resurrected, and since the summer of 1978 has led to a real, wide-ranging, and as yet unchecked cultural revival in the official media.

PROTEST

Movements of protest, demonstrations, wall-posters, manifestations of dissent and even outright opposition and dissidence have not been unknown since the establishment of the People's Republic (PRC) in 1949. Indeed, one could easily chart the development of the PRC in terms of dissent and opposition.[29] Wall-posters – *dazibao*, meaning 'large character posters' in Chinese – have been a characteristic and legitimate form of expression since 1957.[30] Moreover, wall-poster compaigns have often been used in the service of factional interplay and leadership struggles, particularly during the GPCR and the seventies. In 1976, for example, Deng Xiaoping first came under open criticism in wall-posters during January before his eventual dismissal in April. Dissent and dissidence against the CCP and its rule were given an airing in the 'Hundred Flowers' Movement during May and the first week of June 1957.[31] Then, as a result of Mao's policy initiatives of 1956 and 1957 to 'Let a hundred flowers bloom, let a hundred schools of thought contend', intellectuals and the upper strata of non-party society were encouraged to say what they really felt about the new regime, and did. However, criticism of the CCP went far beyond the limits acceptable to the party's leadership and from 8th June on, it counter-attacked with a campaign against the 'Rightists' – those who had spoken out so freely during the previous month. More virulent still were the words and actions of the Red Guards called into being by Mao during the GPCR. Red Guard publications lampooned and degraded 'those in authority taking the Capitalist road',[32] while other Red Guards and the 'Maoist' forces of the GPCR literally 'dragged out' the 'capitalist roaders' and humiliated them in public.

Nor was violent protest confined to the GPCR. In the last years of Mao's life, for example, Mao, those who were later to become known as the 'Gang of Four' (namely Mao's wife, Jiang Qing; and the three leading Shanghai cadres, Zhang Chunqiao, Yao Wenyuan and Wang Hongwen), and the policies they were pursuing became increasingly unpopular. Strikes were reported in Hangzhou, riots in Baoding. In February 1976, Bai Ziqing, a worker in the Chongqing Iron and Steel Works, rapidly became a popular hero in Sichuan province after he had written two wall-posters. The first entitled 'I love the motherland', was posted in Chongqing a few weeks after Zhou Enlai's death (8th January 1976), praised Zhou's policies and criticized Zhou's detractors. The second, posted along with a copy of the first in the main street of Chengdu – the capital of Sichuan province, where Bai had travelled en route to his home town for the Chinese New Year – was more explicit, criticizing Zhang Chunqiao by name. Crowds gathered to read both posters, blocking the street and necessitating police action which quickly degenerated into a riot between supporters and opponents of Bai Ziqing's view, the rival supporters of Zhou and Zhang respectively.[33] But perhaps the best known manifestation of discontent during that period was the 'Tiananmen Incident' of 5th April 1976, when a crowd, demonstrating in memory of Zhou Enlai and against the current leadership, not only filled to overflowing the square mile of Tiananmen Square in the heart of Beijing, but also attacked a public security office, set vehicles alight, physically attacked individuals supposed to be followers of the current radical leaders, and refused to disperse, having to be forcibly expelled (or arrested) from the square by the public security forces.

However, this does not mean either that the fabric of Chinese society has been in constant danger of collapse, or that the leadership of the Communist party-state has ever been seriously weakened. On the contrary, dissent and opposition have often strengthened the leadership's control over society. In the first place, there are different levels of opposition. There may be outright opposition to, and revolt against the regime in toto. There may be opposition by individuals and groups within the leadership, who while accepting the nature of the regime object either on a personal or programmatic basis to current politics. Such individuals and groups may or may not have a wider social basis. There may be individuals and groups outside the leadership, within the politico-administrative system or society at large, who accept the regime, but are opposed to the current leadership and/or its policies, either totally or partially. Finally, there may be opposition to specific individuals or policies without opposition to either the regime or the current leadership in general.[34]

Secondly, there has been an inherent dualism to opposition and dissent in China since 1949. Opposition and dissent have occurred spontaneously, notably before 1954 when the new regime was being consolidated; and in national minority (i.e. ethnically non-Han Chinese) areas such as Tibet where there was a revolt in 1959. However, since 1954, national minority areas apart, opposition and dissent in society at large have occurred almost totally as a result of encouragement by China's leaders, as in the 'Hundred Flowers' Movement of 1957. There is then a sense in which this type of opposition and dissent can be viewed as officially initiated or (government) 'directed'. At least partially this 'directed' opposition and dissent resulted from Mao's emphasis on development through 'struggle' and 'uninterrupted revolution'.[35] But opposition and dissent have also been manipulated by parts of the leadership – and in particular by Mao – to persuade, pressurize, and remove other decision makers, as, for example in Mao's creation of the GPCR and the Red Guards in order to defeat his opponents within the party. Of course, such forces once unleashed cannot always be controlled or contained exactly as their instigators would like, as both the 'Hundred Flowers' Movement and the GPCR demonstrate. None the less there remain important differences between directed and non-directed movements of opposition and dissent, not the least because the former are more easily brought to heel. Directed opposition which originates from the party, the leadership in general, or a specific leader can always be defused by a change of heart at the centre, as in the 'Hundred Flowers' Movement or with the Red Guard movement during the GPCR. On the other hand, non-directed opposition is much less easily controlled by the party or leadership, not only by definition, but also because it develops its own momentum and organization however informal and weak. For example, the famous Li Yizhe poster 'Concerning Socialist Democracy and the Legal System', which first appeared on a Canton Wall in 1974, was still a major issue during the Democracy Movement despite, or perhaps because of, the arrest of its authors, and an official campaign to rebut their attack.[36] In the meantime their ideas, which were a somewhat Djilas-like critique of the PRC, had spread throughout China through the production and distribution of duplicated copies of the poster.

The Democracy Movement has much in common with previous movements of opposition and dissent. Like the GPCR, although on a much smaller scale, it has produced its own 'mass organizations' and unofficial publications. Like the 'Hundred Flowers' Movement of 1957, a major theme of the Democracy Movement has been cultural democracy. Wall-posters, magazines and newspapers, demonstrations have been the techniques of opposition and dissent that have evolved since 1949. On the other hand, the Democracy Movement has also differed greatly from its predecessors. Unlike the 'Hundred Flowers' it has not been a movement of intellectuals, who have, for the most part, been disparaging about its activities. Nor, like the 'Hundred Flowers' did it develop into an outright attack on the regime. The level of opposition was in general very low indeed. There were those like Wei Jingsheng of 'Exploration', and Li Jiahua of 'Thaw' who were opposed completely to the existence of the PRC, but in the main Democracy Movement activists pledged themselves to Marxism-Leninism (and even on occasion Mao Zedong Thought), party rule, and the current leadership.[37] Where there was opposition, it was mainly to the past or to specific leaders and policies. In particular, Wang Dongxing was 'public enemy number one' as far as the Democracy Movement was concerned. Unlike the Red Guards, the Democracy Movement was not based on student activists. There were the odd few students involved with 'The Spring of Peking', 'April 5th Forum', and the group working under the pseudonym Gong Nianzhou – *Gong* is a surname and *nianzhou* means 'remember Zhou Enlai' – which produced 'Science, Democracy and Law' from the China Traditional Opera College. But for the most part activists were workers, aged between 25 and 35. Nor are the Democracy Movement's publications like the Red Guard publications of the previous decade. Paradoxically, there is more emphasis on cultural change and development in the former than in those dating from the GPCR, which were mainly narrowly political. Moreover, whereas many Red Guard publications had some degree of official support (if only that of a powerful individual) and were printed, those from the Democracy Movement had none. Indeed this distinction highlights a unique aspect of the Democracy Movement in the history of the PRC. Excluding national minority areas and the period immediately after 1949 when the new regime was consolidating its hold (a process which can be said to have been completed by 1954) the Democracy Movement is the only example of a non-directed movement of opposition and dissent. The leadership, or individual leaders may well have tried to use or manipulate the Democracy Movement once it had started, but there is nothing to suggest that it was in any sense an officially initiated movement.

Superficially, the Democracy Movement would also appear to have much in common with opposition and dissent in the Soviet Union and Eastern Europe. There are similar preoccupations with civil rights and cultural democracy, and the emergence of an unofficial press. However, there is an important difference between, on the one hand, the Soviet and East European dissent movements, and on the other, the Chinese Democracy Movement, quite apart from the obvious youth of the latter. Whereas dissent in Communist Europe can for the most part be regarded as both anti-regime and 'underground', this is not the case for the Democracy Movement during at least the first five months of its existence. Unlike *samizdat* literature the publications of the Democracy Movement were sold openly on the streets of Beijing, rather than being passed from hand to hand or copied in secret. A notice of publication would appear, often on Democracy Wall and as much as a week in advance, saying when and where a journal or newspaper would be on sale. As with most of the Democracy Movement's activities during the period covered here, there was little attempt at secrecy and seemingly little need. Although the Democracy Movement never had official backing or gained official acceptance – those unofficial publications which tried to pay income tax on their takings or to register as newspapers with the postal services were not permitted to do so – its activities were not criticized by the national leadership until mid-March 1979, and Deng Xiaoping had seemed to be at least moderately in favour at the end of November 1978.[38] For their part, far from feeling themselves anti-regime or part of an 'underground', the vast majority of Democracy Movement activists, as already mentioned, felt themselves to be pro-regime and supportive of the contemporary leadership in general. It may have been a naive feeling but it was none the less genuine for that.

It was precisely in order to distance themselves from the accusation that they constituted an 'underground', that the Democracy Movement's activities referred to themselves as 'mass organizations'[39] and to their publications as either 'unofficial' (*feiguanfang*), or 'popular' (*minjian*) literature, or more generally as 'mimeographed publications' (*youyin kanwu*).[40] Although, naturally enough this did not stop the accusations being made; as for example in a circular of the Beijing Party Committee, which was reproduced in a wall-poster (dated 23rd January 1979) on Democracy Wall.[41] In fact, the Democracy Movement occupied the grey areas between the legal and the illegal, between official or private activities (that is of individuals, collectives, or other officially-recognized social units) and those which are most definitely 'underground'. It was this ambiguity, in a period when the rule of law and equality before the law were being officially stressed, that created problems for both the Democracy Movement's activities and the CCP's leadership.

POETRY AND THE UNOFFICIAL PRESS

As mentioned in the Preface, the aim of this book is to present an anthology of poetry from Beijing's Democracy Movement during the winter of 1978/9, and at the same time to sketch the development of the movement from November 1978 to April 1979. To the Western observer poetry may well seem an odd choice of focus. However, poetry has in fact been an integral part of the Democracy Movement's activities – on the streets of Beijing, on Democracy Wall, and in the unofficial press which emerged. In general, this may well have been because poetry is both more popular in China than in the West, and also traditionally more political. Petitioners to the Emperor might well have couched their requests in poetry. Peasants complaining about present conditions in China's countryside, urban workers concerned with housing, or 'educated youth' – school and university graduates from the

B

urban areas sent down to the countryside because of employment and population pressures – wanting to return home, all might well do the same today. Long queues form at bookshops on the tenth of each month when 'Poetry Monthly' (*Shikan* – an official magazine published by the People's Literature Publishing House in Beijing) usually appears and it almost invariably sells out within a few days; and when wall-posters are displayed those which are presented as (or include) poetry generally attract the biggest crowds.

More specifically, poetry has been an integral part of the Democracy Movement because its genesis dates back to the Tiananmen Incident of 1976 and the role of poetry then. At that time, when the people of Beijing demonstrated against the later-to-become 'Gang of Four' and for the late Zhou Enlai and his policies, they not only came to Tiananmen Square with wreaths, but they showed their protest through poetry. It was, to a large extent, the Beijing Party Committee's decision in mid-November 1978[42] to reverse the verdict on the 1976 incident as a 'counter-revolutionary incident', which is what it had been called at the time,[43] and now to describe it as a 'completely revolutionary event' which provided the spark for the Democracy Movement. Moreover, it was announced that books of poetry from the April 5 Movement (the date of the 1976 incident) which had been circulating privately for some time – such as those produced by the Beijing No. 2 Foreign Languages Institute and the 7th Ministry of Machine Building[44] – supposedly for internal circulation only, were now to be published officially without restrictions on their distribution with Chairman Hua's calligraphy for the title of one of the volumes.[45] It seemed indeed to be a sign of the times on the 16th November 1978, when, as soon as the news broke that the verdict on the 1976 Tiananmen Incident had been reversed, a bus full of 'Tiananmen Poetry' was parked on the pavement at Xidan (in front of what was later to become Democracy Wall) selling previously private and restricted books of poems.

For both general and specific reasons then, poetry has

played a significant role in the Democracy Movement. Poems have been declaimed in the open air to those who will listen, they have been written on wall-posters and stuck up in public, and most important in terms of greater communication they have been published in the unofficial publications of the Democracy Movement. Although 'Science, Democracy and Law', which produced a regular digest of posters appearing on Democracy Wall, devoted 26 of 32 pages in its first issue to poetry, approximately a third of all that was produced (or reproduced) in the unofficial publications during the winter 1978/9 was poetry. No matter what kind of publication, be it the more political or the 'just' literary, almost all included poetry to a greater or lesser extent.

Eighty-four individual issues of some twenty-seven titles were unofficially published from the start of the Democracy Movement until 4th May 1979, although only about twelve titles were regularly produced during that period.[46] It is from those publications that the poems appearing in this volume have been selected. The selection has been made in order to provide a representative sample of the poetry appearing in the Democracy Movement's unofficial press, rather than necessarily for their literary merit. Many, of course have been selected for both, but for a few in the final analysis, naivety, narrowness of vision, and even on occasion lack of something one might call 'poetic grace' have been put aside and it is 'interest value' which has counted highest.

The rest of the book is arranged chronologically, with the poems appearing at the end of the chapter where they are most suited thematically, rather than according to when they were published. This method of presentation has been adopted not least because neither poetry nor unofficial magazines and newspapers can be produced overnight, requiring a great deal of foresight, preparation and planning. Indeed, many of the poems presented here were written and secreted or clandestinely distributed among friends during the decade 1966-76, and for many if a poem dated from those years then somehow it grew in stature.

By way of example, this introduction ends with (as far as is known) the earliest poem in this book, having been written in 1962, and one which clearly shows the importance of the relationship between literature and politics – a theme which runs repeatedly through the Democracy Movement's poetry. This poem is essentially a social and political satire, and one of undoubted historical importance. The self-descriptions of various animals are used to caricature individuals or social groups in a kind of verbal cartoon. A literal translation of its title is 'A Collection of Animals' and it is clearly based on an earlier idea of 1957. Then in January, Liu Shahe had written and published a similar anthropomorphic 'Collection of Flowers and Trees' in a Sichuan province literary magazine (*Xingxing shikan*). Accepted at the time, after the end of the 'Hundred Flowers' Movement of 1957 and the start of the campaign against 'Rightism' and 'Rightists' which followed, Liu Shake's poem was officially denounced retrospectively as one of the first and major blasts of the 'Rightist movement'. Given both its political antecedents and its content – for example, no Chinese would fail to equate Mao Zedong with The Braying Donkey, since the donkey is the symbol of Mao's home province, Hunan, and Mao had engaged in 'self-criticism' at a Central Work Conference in 1961[47] – 'Animal Crackers' was immediately criticized in 1962 as 'counter-revolutionary'. The author, the famous artist Huang Yongyu (who used the pseudonym here of Yong Yu, the characters being homophones for his real personal name) was criticized again in 1964, and was later severely punished during the Cultural Revolution. As far as is known, although criticized the poem had never been published. Huang Yongyu, now in his mid-fifties, has recently been rehabilitated, and during March/April 1979 had a one-man exhibition of his work (mainly oil paintings) at the Fine Arts Museum in Beijing. The May issue of the official 'Poetry Monthly' (No. 5, 1979) carried a selection of his other poetry, and he was featured in an article in the July 1979 issue of *China Reconstructs*.[48]

ANIMAL CRACKERS
Yong Yu

A Moth:
>Hey man! Just listen –
>Take heed of what I've done.
>Don't go mistaking every candle for the sun.

A Donkey on a treadmill:
>Isn't it hard! It's a wonder, they say
>I'm really getting somewhere,
>I walk a thousand miles each day.

A Centipide:
>At first I thought
>That with more pairs of feet
>I could walk faster at a snappy beat ...

A Camel:
>If I've but one virtue
>– I'll tell you it for free –
>I look down my nose at hardship,
>It just doesn't bother me.

A Horse:
>Ford and Toyota, Mercedes and Shanghai,
>They've deprived me of my honour,
>So I hate them passing by.

A Cuckoo:
>When I call you in the morning,
>I'll wake you early on.
>Then while I lie in the cool shade,
>You can labour in the sun.

A Spider:
>I've built a superstructure,
>Nothing does it bear
>But the bodies of the careless
>Who've wandered into there.

An Oyster:
>   However small the problem,
>   Be careful what you do;
>   Remember that small problems
>   Can lead to big ones too.

A Flounder:
>   I moved both my eyes to the same side of my face,
>   More clearly to pry into others' disgrace.
>   Things seen so clearly are bound to be true,
>   Now no one can challenge my one-sided view.

A Scorpion:
>   When your eyes are on me
>   I'm a dependable friend and true.
>   But turn your back an instant
>   And I'm the first who's after you.

A Sparrow:
>   Other people's petty defects,
>   Other people's weary lives
>   Make me burst into singing,
>   Make my vocal chords alive.

A Braying Donkey:
>   I'm not satisfied with peoples'
>   Assessment of my voice.
>   I have to bray still louder;
>   I simply have no choice.

A Hen:
>   I've done something! I've done something!
>   Of that there is no doubt.
>   I can't help being excited
>   I want to scream and shout.

A Cicada:
>   One final performance
>   One final fling,
>   I've prepared all my life
>   For this one chance to sing.

A Crow:
> "One for sorrow" 's what people say,
> And if I only crow once
> They'll claim an unlucky day.

A Cricket:
> Schumann says 'A musical race
> Ends in a complete retreat,
> Or else complete embrace.'

A Bed Bug:
> When you see me
> If you want to
> You can kill.
> But remember, Mister
> It's your blood
> You'll spill.

A Bookworm:
> Who says that I've no theory?
> It can't be true, why look
> I've inwardly digested
> Many a useful book.

A Cat:
> My tongue's so clever
> So adaptable you see
> That there's no way
> To dish the dirt on me.

A Grasshopper:
> Give my neck just one little prod
> I'll cry for mercy
> And nod and nod and nod.

A Bee:
> Regardless of struggle, regardless of strife,
> One loses one's weapon
> One loses one's life.

A Clam:

> A weak master depends on solid gates
> I always live behind closed doors
> I am my own master but
> I live in secret, like a thief.

A Louse:

> I'm a very friendly fellow,
> But please, make no mistake,
> I only want to be with people
> I don't care what line they take.

A Leech:

> Hello old chap! Nice to see you again.
> Now let me own – I won't pretend –
> I do so want to be close friends.

A Pelican:

> With my beak
> As everyone knows
> I'll handle anything that goes.

A Sheep:

> As I stroll around the town,
> I'm always very careful of my gown,
> So I don't ruin people's future sheepskin coats.

A Parrot:

> I always echo people's words though
> What they mean
> I never know.

A Giraffe:

> The upper class
> Is where it's at,
> It's not convenient
> To be lower than that.

A Hippopotamus:

> You can say what you will
> I don't mind.
> My big mouth's my advantage, I find.

An Ape:
> Man, why are you so haughty?
> What makes you think you're great?
> Can you crawl around on all fours
> As well as standing straight?

An Ostrich:
> People created the legend
> That I bury my head in the sand.
> Then they buried their heads in that myth:
> Will they never understand?

A Crab:
> Aren't people funny? Aren't they strange?
> They always walk straight ahead.
> Have they never thought of walking
> Sideways instead?

from *Today*, No. 1, p. 33/4.

Notes

Most of the animals described here have much the same connotations in China as in the West. Two, however, perhaps require a little further explanation. Traditionally, Crickets in China have been caught and used to fight each other in much the same way as fighting cocks. Particularly in the modern period the Crab has become the symbol for a tyrant. Thus during the Japanese occupation, the famous Chinese painter Qi Baishi, painted many pictures of crabs.

References

[1] See for example Arlette Laduguie, 'The Human Rights Movement' in *Index on Censorship* Vol. 9, No. 1, February 1980, p. 18.

[2] 'Joint Statement of 25th January 1979' in *Tansuo* ('Exploration') No. 2, 29 January 1979, p. 16.

[3] See p. 103.

[4] A full translation may be found in United States, Joint Publications Research Services (JPRS) 73756, 26 June 1979, p. 7-23.

[5] ibid., p. 19.

[6] See for example, *Renmin ribao* (*People's Daily*) (RMRB) 21 January 1975, p. 1.

[7] A full translation may be found in *Index on Censorship* Vol. 8, No. 5, p. 3.

[8] *Summary of World Broadcasts, Part III, The Far East* (SWB FE) 5975/BII/1-3. Kyodo in English 20 November 1978 and Agence France Press (AFP) in English 20 November 1978.

[9] Wall-poster on Democracy Wall, 29 November 1978.

[10] For example wall-poster at crossroads of Xidan and Changan Jie, 2 December 1978.

[11] For example, see: SWB FE/6009/BII/15, Kyodo in English, 3 January 1979. All three were in fact removed from office by the 5th Plenum of the 11th Central Committee in February 1980, see *Beijing review*, No. 10, 1980.

[12] Lu Min, 'Do away with the power of administrative leadership of basic level party organizations in factories, mines and other enterprises', in *Beijing zhi chun* ('The Spring of Peking') No. 2, 27 January 1979, p. 17.

[13] 'On Human Rights' in *Qimeng (Guiyang)* (Enlightenment, Guiyang Branch in Beijing) No. 3, 1 January 1979, p. 11-27. The article appears unsigned but was in fact written by one of the men who later went on to establish *Jiedong* ('Thaw').

[14] 'Further Discussion of whether the United States is "A Democratic Paradise" – a talk with Jie Jun', in *Siwu Luntan* ('April 5th Forum') No. 9, 29 April 1979, p. 15.

[15] For example, see Lu Min, op. cit., p. 19.

[16] Lu Min, 'Gradually abolish the bureaucratic system and establish a democratic system modelled on the Paris Commune', in 'The Spring of Peking' No 1, 8 January 1979, 17-21 – No. 2, 27 January 1979, p. 43-45.
During the GPCR (in 1967), Shanghai had responded to Mao's call 'to seize power from below' by establishing a commune. This became a leftist deviation as Mao made plain in a conversation with Zhang Chunqiao and Yao Wenyuan. See *Mao Tse-Tung Unrehearsed*, (ed.) Stuart R. Schram, (Penguin, Harmondsworth, Middx 1974), p. 278.

[17] The title 'The Spring of Peking' has been adopted throughout this book as the translation of *Beijing zhi chun*, rather than the more elegant 'Beijing Spring', because this is precisely the translation its producers themselves have constantly used on its cover. See p. 85.

[18] For example, *Huohua* ('The Spark') the only issue of which appared in late March 1979.

[19] *Siwu bao* (April 5th) p. 2, on Democracy Wall 26 November 1978. See Appendix 2, p. 159.

[20] 'To the Reader' by *Jintian bianjibu* (Today Editorial Board), *Jintian* ('Today/The Moment') No. 1, p. 2. See Appendix 2, p. 162.

[21] p. 109.

[22] 'Statement of the Human Rights Alliance' in *Zhongguo Renquan* ('China's Human Rights') No. 1, February 1979, p. 7.

[23] 'April 5th Forum' No. 9, op. cit., p. 15.

[24] 'Today/The Moment' No. 1, p. 2, op. cit. See p. 296.

[25] This particular quotation is from 'The Spring of Peking' No. 1, p. 2, 'Publication Statement'. See Appendix 2, p. 161.

[26] 'Let a hundred flowers blossom, a hundred schools of thought contend!' Lu Dingyi (Director, CCP Propaganda Department) 26 May 1956, in Bowie and Fairbank (eds), *Communist China 1955-1959* (Harvard University Press, Cambridge, Mass. 1965), p. 153.

[27] *Selected Works of Mao Zedong* (SW) Vol 5, (Foreign Languages Press, Beijing, 1977), p. 408.

[28] See for example: Lois Wheeler Snow, *China on Stage*, (Random House, New York, 1972).

[29] Peter R. Moody, *Opposition and Dissent in Contemporary China*, (Hoover Institution, Stanford, California, 1977) especially Ch. 6 'Opposition Movements' p. 157-236.

[30] In 1958 Mao Zedong said 'Big-character posters are an extremely useful new weapon ... they have widely come into use. They must be employed for all occasions', in RMRB 17 July 1958, p. 5.

[31] R. Macfarquhar, *The Hundred Flowers Campaign and the Chinese Intellectuals* (Praeger, New York, 1960).

[32] See, for example, p. 75.

[33] Bai Ziqing was arrested shortly after the Tiananmen Incident at the beginning of April 1976, but was released from custody in November 1978.

[34] For a useful discussion of opposition in Communist Party States, see H. Gordon Skilling, 'Background to the study of opposition in Communist Eastern Europe' in *Government and Opposition* Vol 3, No. 3, Summer 1968, p. 297-301.

[35] For an excellent discussion, see Stuart R. Schram, 'Mao Tse-Tung and the Theory of Permanent Revolution' in *The China Quarterly* (CQ) No. 46, p. 221.

[36] *Li* Zhengtian, Chen *Yi*yang and Huang Xi*zhe*. For an account and analysis see Susan L. Shirk '"Going against the Tide": Political

Dissent in China' in *Survey* Vol. 24, No. 1, p. 82-114. The original can be found in translation in *Issues and Studies* (*Taipei*) Vol. XII, No. 1, p. 110-149.

[37] See, for example, the introductory editorials in Appendix 2.

[38] See p. 63.

[39] 'Joint Statement of 25th January 1979', op. cit.

[40] See, for example, 'April 5th Forum' No. 1 where a number of different terms are used.

[41] *Daily Telegraph* (London), 24th January 1979.

[42] RMRB 16 November 1978.

[43] *Peking Review* No 15 (1976), 9 April 1976, p. 4.

[44] Beijing No. 2 Foreign Languages Institute, *Tiananmen shiwenji* ('A collection of Tiananmen Poems') and 7th Ministry of Machine Building, *Geming Shichao* ('Revolutionary Poetry').

[45] *Tiananmen shichao* ('A selection of Tiananmen poems'), (*Renminwenxue chubanshe*, Beijing, 1978).
The other two were *Geming shichao* ('Revolutionary Poetry') (*Zhongguo quingnian chubanshe*, Beijing 1979), and *Tiananmen geming shiwenxuan* ('A Selection of Tiananmen Revolutionary Poetry') (*Beijing chubanshe*, Beijing, 1979).

[46] See Appendix 4, Beijing's Unofficial Press, p. 298 ff. 4th May has been chosen as the cut-off point not only because it is a national holiday and anniversary of the May 4th Movement but also because in Beijing it, together with May 1st (Workers Day), provides a convenient holiday to divide summer from winter.

[47] K. Lieberthal, *Research Guide to Central Party and Government Meetings in China, 1949-1975* (International Arts and Science Press, New York, 1976) Meeting 154, p. 171.

[48] *China Reconstructs* Vol. 28, No. 8, August 1979, p. 37. 'The paintings of Huang Yongyu' by Primerose Gigliesi. His poetry appeared in *Shi Kan* ('Poetry Monthly') Beijing. No. 5, 1979, p. 52.

CHAPTER TWO

The Democracy Movement: Origins and Roots

Cover of 'April 5th Forum', No. 8

THE APRIL 5TH MOVEMENT

The immediate origins of the Democracy Movement lie in the April 5th Movement. April 4th 1976 was the Qing Ming (Sweeping of the Graves) Festival – a traditional day for remembering the dead. Since the establishment of the People's Republic it had also been a particular remembrance day for 'revolutionary martyrs'. Earlier in the year, on 8th January 1976, Zhou Enlai, more familiarly known as 'Premier Zhou', had died. On 19th March, the first wreaths to Premier Zhou's memory were placed on the Revolutionary Martyrs' Memorial in the centre of Tiananmen Square: a monument incidentally whose inscription is written in Zhou's calligraphy. Other wreaths followed and on 30th March, the first poems and eulogies appeared. From then until Qing Ming, crowds flocked to the square bringing wreaths, flowers and poems until the base of the monument was quite literally overflowing. However, on the evening of April 4th, the public security forces moved in and cleared everything away from the memorial. The square was cordoned off by lines of public security officials on the morning of April 5th, but not unnaturally this heavy handed approach was counter-productive. The crowds who came to the square were far angrier and incensed than those who had surrounded the memorial previously. They brought new wreaths and poems, which were much more explicitly against the current leadership of Jiang Qing (Mao's wife) and Shanghai's three leading cadres, Zhang Chunqiao, Yao Wenyuan, and Wang Hongwen, rather than 'just' praising Zhou, which could be construed only as an implicit attack on the erstwhile 'Gang of Four', For example:

TO A CERTAIN WOMAN[1]

You must be mad
To want to be an empress!
Here's a mirror to look at yourself
And see what you really are.
You've got together a little gang
To stir up trouble all the time,
Hoodwinking the people, capering about.
But your days are numbered.
Mao Zedong Thought lights the way,
Guides our hearts
To discern true from false.
You can never fool us!
The Premier's memory, glorious as sun and moon,
Will warm our hearts a thousand years.
His last drop of lifeblood was shed for the people,
The power of his name will last ten thousand years.
Whoever dares oppose our Premier
Is like a mad dog barking at the sun –
Wake up to reality!

The demonstrators broke through the public security lines, placed their new wreaths, posted their new poems and were generally more belligerent. Authors were hoisted on high to declaim their poems, eulogies of Zhou, or condemnations of Jiang Qing et. al. The crowd rushed the Great Hall of the People (to the west of the Square), overturned several official vehicles and set them on fire, and sacked a public security office in the south east corner of Tiananmen Square. Moreover, the crowd – which spilt out of the square and along adjacent streets – refused to disperse, even when Wu De, the city's Mayor, broadcast an appeal over the loudspeaker system. Eventually, after nightfall, the public security forces were sent in to break up the crowd. Several hundreds were arrested immediately,[2] and it is not known how many were summarily executed, although most estimates vary around two to four hundred. Moreover, others were arrested in the following days, and on April 7th, the 'Tiananmen Incident' as it had now become, was described as a 'Counter-revolutionary Incident'. At the same time the inheritor of Zhou Enlai's mantle and almost by definition, the inner-leadership opposition to Jiang Qing and company, Deng Xiaoping, was dismissed from his leadership positions in party and state,[3] and in effect held responsible for the breakdown of public order.

At the time, the demonstrators had barely dwelt on the parallels with the manifestations of May 4th 1919. Then, students and intellectuals concerned with China's political, economic, and cultural national regeneration, had demonstrated in Tiananmen Square against both the Versailles Treaty and the Chinese Government's acquiescence to Japanese occupation of Shandong province, which had previously belonged to the Germans. The demonstration developed into a riot and several student leaders were arrested, thus escalating the conflict. The incident occurred during a period of great intellectual change in China, based on the rejection of traditional values and the greater acceptance of Western ideas – 'Mr. Democracy and Mr. Science' in Chen Duxiu's words – and has come to give its name to the period from about 1915 to the mid-1920's as the 'May 4th Movement.'[4] The May 4th Movement has its place in the CCP's history because along with the acceptance of other Western ideas by groups and individuals in China came Marxism, the involvement of the Comintern, and the eventual establishment of the CCP in 1921.

However, as time passed, and particularly after Mao's death (in September 1976), and the fall of the 'Gang of Four' (in October), the Tiananmen Incident of April 5th 1976 became known unofficially as a symbol both of resistance to the 'Gang of Four' and their policies, and of potential national regeneration under a new leadership, as the April 5th Movement. Some of the parallels with the May 4th Movement are obvious, or were made so. Thus both involved demonstrations in Tiananmen Square and were concerned

with national regeneration. Where the slogan of the May 4th
Movement had been 'Democracy and Science', the April 5th
Movement in its critique of late-Maoist China as feudal,
fascist, and lawless, added a third element – law. Thus,
'Science, Democracy and Law' became the goals of
modernization, as well as providing the title for an unofficial
publication emanating from the China Traditional Opera
College in Beijing. Moreover, the two movements are
inherently linked through a word play in Chinese. In Chinese
there are no names for the months of the solar year, merely
numbers. Thus April is 4, and May 5. The May 4th
Movement is therefore known as the '5.4 Movement' (*wusi
yundong*) and the April 5th Movement as '4.5 Movement', (*siwu
yundong*).

As a movement, before November 1978, the April 5th
Movement was even more diffuse than the Democracy
Movement was to become, although it existed at all levels of
Chinese society. Apart from being a symbol of opposition to
the policies officially implemented in the mid-1970s, its main
purpose – according to both official and unofficial sources –
seems to have been the preservation of the poems presented on
April 5th in Tiananmen Square, or on similar occasions
around the country. As Xiao Lan writes in his introduction to
the English edition of the official version of 'The Tiananmen
Poems':

> Risking imprisonment, thousands had managed to preserve
> the poems they had copied or the photographs they had
> taken at the Square by concealing them in flowerpots,
> hollowed-out candles, the linings of coal stoves, or burying
> them in the countryside.[5]

Moreover, after the leadership changes in the autumn of 1976,
plans were put in motion to publish 'The Tiananmen Poems'
privately. Several versions duly appeared during 1977 and
early 1978, as for example the volume entitled 'Revolutionary
Poetry' (*Geming shichao*) published by a department of the 7th
Ministry of Machine Building, or 'A Collection of Tiananmen
Poetry' (*Tiananmen shiwenji*) produced by the Beijing No. 2
Foreign Languages Institute.

However, on 15th November 1978 the 1976 verdict on the Tiananmen Incident as a 'counter-revolutionary incident' was reversed by the Beijing Party Committee so that it now became 'a completely revolutionary event'.[6] In the wake of this decision the April 5th Movement became 'officialized' and explicit parallels were drawn with the May 4th Movement.[7] Whereas the May 4th Movement was, as before, regarded as the birth of modern nationalism and democracy, the April 5th Movement was now said to be the birth of 'socialist democracy'. In effect, the 'officialization' of the April 5th Movement legitimized the near hundred and eighty degree turn in policies that had been implemented in the period since Mao's death, by reference to the popular will:

> ... this movement, unprecedented in scale declared to the whole world that China did not belong to the 'Gang of Four'. The people and the people alone decide the destiny of China and determine the advance of history ... Who organized the April events in Tiananmen Square? The people. Who directed these events? The people ... ... The April 1976 struggle knelled the hour of the 'Gang of Four' and awakened the hundreds of millions, which is the most important condition for Chairman Hua leading the nation in October to victoriously smashing the 'Gang of Four'.[8]

But it was also this 'officialization' which provided the spark to ignite the Democracy Movement.

SOCIAL AND ORGANIZATIONAL ORIGINS

Although the groups and publications of the Democracy Movement were conscious of, and certainly tried to capitalize on, parallels with the May 4th Movement, in fact they had their own distinctive features which resulted from the more recent history of April 5th 1976 and the GPCR. In the first place, the Democracy Movement was not, as the May 4th Movement had been, inspired by university students. As has already been mentioned most of the Democracy Movement's activists were workers, not students. If they were ordinary workers this would say a great deal for the PCR's levels of cultural attainment. However, with a few exceptions (notably again in 'The Spring of Peking'[9]) they were not.

Perhaps the most amazing aspect of the Democracy Movement, other than that it occurred at all, is the relatively homogenous social background of its activists. For the most part they were the sons and daughters of the middle and upper-middle strata of Chinese society. They were the children of cadres and intellectuals who prior to the GPCR would have expected to gain some tertiary education, but because of the educational policies of the Cultural Revolution were 'sent down to the front line of production' instead of the possibility of attending institutes of higher education. They might have had the right academic qualifications, but they certainly had the wrong 'class' background, that is parents who were either in disgrace or under suspicion during the GPCR. But precisely because their parents had held privileged positions before 1966 and were 'well-connected' they were able to ensure that their children, instead of being 'sent down to the countryside' to work, went to work at the 'front line of production' in suburban communes or urban factories and workshops. Aged between roughly 25 and 35 in 1978, a very few would have had the chance to return to higher eduction by passing the national university entrance examinations, but the majority would not, and it is quite clear that even those who did return to study were disadvantaged, both accidentally and deliberately.[10]

The two editors of 'Exploration' which has received much official publicity recently are excellent examples of the Democracy Movement activist. Wei Jingsheng, sentenced to fifteen years and branded as a 'counter revolutionary' for eighteen (and so deprived of his civil rights) was an electrician at the Beijing Zoo. His father is a cadre in the CCP in Beijing, and a deputy director of a department in a central ministry. At the start of the GPCR in 1966 he had belonged to a group of what were then known as the 'Old Red Guards' – that is the first Red Guard Units to be mobilized, often the children of the privileged cadres. Yang Guang, his collaborator on

'Exploration' was somewhat younger, a student at the Workers' University and a classmate of Hua Guofeng's daughter with whom he did not see exactly eye to eye. His father is a relatively high cadre and engineer in the Ministry of Light Industry. In terms of social background, if not of political stance, they are typical of the Democracy Movement's activists. Others are the children of the pre-1966 privileged cadres and intellectuals. Indeed, if there are distinctions to be made within the Democracy Movement's activists, it is that the children of cadres have drifted to the more political activities and publications, such as 'The Spring of Peking'; whereas the children of intellectuals have been more concerned with cultural democracy and been drawn more to publications like 'Today'.

The groups and publications which were an essential part of the Democracy Movement, no more came into existence overnight than were collections of poetry produced from thin air. In the same way that many of the poems (and particularly those at the end of this section) were written throughout the early and mid-1970's and only saw the public light of day once the Democracy Movement had started, so too did various informal groups of friends and acquaintances. In many cases there were groups of people who had met at their workplace. Thus, for example, a large proportion of 'Today's' editorial board worked, or had worked at, one of Beijing's Building and Construction Companies. In some cases, people had known each other since the GPCR and their Red Guard days, as had those who formed the core of 'Exploration', having been part of a Red Guard organization called 'Prepare' who were opposed to Jiang Qing, had gone to Canton in December 1966, and were imprisoned for three months for their trouble. But by far the commonest experience which had brought people together had been the Tiananmen Incident of 1976. The most easily documented case is that of the leaders of 'The Spring of Peking', who in the wake of the 'officialization' of the April 5th Movement received a great deal of official national publicity for having been persecuted in April 1976. Thus

many of these were mentioned in the newly revised official
account of the Tiananmen Incident,[11] and other accounts of
persecution at that time[12] which were published in late 1978.
Such publicity implies connections and it is no small wonder
then that other Democracy Movement activists regarded those
who were in 'The Spring of Peking' as 'the children of the
aristocracy' (*guizu de haizi*).

The origins of the unofficial press lie not so much in the
April 5th Movement or the GPCR as in the Democracy
Movement itself. The practice of producing mimeographed
copies of wall-posters in order to gain a wider dissemination
for one's ideas dates back at least to 1974 and the Li Yizhe
poster on 'Socialist Democracy and the Legal System'.
During the GPCR, Red Guards had access to both printing
and duplicating facilities; while during Qing Ming 1976,
people came to Tiananmen Square to copy the poems down
for themselves. Very early on in the Democracy Movement on
26th November, one of the first 'mass organizations' to
emerge, the 'April 5th Study Group' (later to become the
'April 5th Forum') proposed in a poster on Democracy Wall
that there should be an unofficial press 'to publish the people's
thoughts and words, which for all kinds of reasons are not
contained in official publications'.[13] It was a suggestion which
needed little encouragement to grow. Only time and finance
were limiting factors. Sometimes wall-posters appeared in
unofficial publications – sometimes unofficial publications
were posted on walls and buildings. By February each group
had a paper, each paper had become a 'group'. Thus, for
example, the 'April 5th Study Group' first produced a paper
as a wall-poster called 'April 5th', (*Siwu bao*). They were then
joined by a group (of one) called 'The People's Forum'
(*Renmin luntan*) and together they produced the 'April 5th
Forum', a name which continued even after January 1979
when the original member of 'The People's Forum' branched
out on his own. He later joined 'Exploration'.

PAEAN TO QING MING

At the Qing Ming Festival
Fine rain falls softly.
Before the Monument to the People's Heroes
Visitors are gathering.
With impassioned words
State your concern for present politics.
For the state of the country
Every man has responsibility.
Fast approaching death
Are the four traitors who disordered the country.
The people will ever regret
The dregs of the old society
Covering up their mistakes,
Refusing to admit their guilt.
The opportunists and the cover-up factions,
That is neglected virtue.

Birds of a feather ...
Still entrenched in high positions,
Still riding about in 'Red Flag' limousines.
You scoundrels
Deep-rooted old social forces
Four puppets dancing to the same tune
Evil practices should be stamped out.
How can crafty sycophants be tolerated,
Enriching themselves and despoiling the country?
Faced with this situation,
The people should impeach public officials!
The people are the motive force.
The history of mankind,
The fate of the country
Should be the people's choice!

The Fifth of April
Glows in splendour
And China's peoples
Are immortalized in the annals of history.
Blood does not flow in vain;
How can heads fall lightly?
It makes the people
Sharp-eyed and discerning.
Before the monument to the People's Heroes
Blood bursts forth again and again.
Under the Founding Flag
Flames rage time after time:
To fight for people's rights,
To punish the traitors,
To warn China,
Autocracy ruins the country!

We will carry out
Premier Zhou's last will.
China's eight hundred million
Dedicate themselves to the country.
Advance wave upon wave,
Cherish it fiercely.
Evil must be stamped out to the last,
A fight to the death.
Scan the whole globe;
The trend of the times
Is democratic rights:
How can we tolerate being deprived of them?
The truth is clear,
Be ready to shed your blood
As martyrs to the cause.
Send forth this song of praise!

from *Grass on the Plain* No. 2, p. 1.

Notes

Grass on the Plain takes its title from a classical poem which is quoted
on its cover:

Far, far away the grass on the plain,
Withers each year to grow again.
Prairie fires first rage without end,
Then spring winds rise up fresh life to sustain.*

Over half its second issue, from which this and the following two
poems are taken, was devoted to poetry written at the time of, or
focusing on, the Tiananmen Incident of April 5th 1976.

RETURN TO TIANANMEN SQUARE

The sacrifice over – all's spilt in the dust,
And today in the Square the raised banner blows.
Red blood and fresh flowers at the foot of the shrine,
Defiant and angry, who dares to oppose?

Standing solemn, our thoughts turn on grief without end,
As recompense for that loss all our tears vainly flow.
Heaven too has a heart, and in sadness grows old,
Flowers thick on the pine wall, like blossoms of snow.

October 1976.

from *Grass on the Plain* No. 2, p. 2.

Notes

The Tiananmen Incident of 1976 centred on the Revolutionary
Martyrs' Memorial, in the middle of the square, where the
demonstrators gathered to lay garlands and wreaths to Zhou Enlai's
memory. It is surrounded by a low hedge of small evergreen bushes.
It is not known how many died when the demonstration was forcibly
broken up, but estimates range from two to four hundred, including
those summarily executed shortly afterwards.

---

* Bai Juyi, *Fude guinan cao guanbie*, in *Tangshi biecaiji* (*Zhonghua shuju*,
Beijing 1975) reprint of 1763 edition, p. 168.

'PUT DOWN THE WINE-CUP, FRIEND'
Rou Huo

Put down the wine-cup, friend! Do not drink again.
I know of your suffering, days torment-ridden,
The door to joy shut in your face, ever hidden,
The smooth road gives warning: 'Passage forbidden'.
Here is an arrogant spirit, and once
In the distance shone fanciful stars in the dawn.
But Fate, like Spring's cold wave's yet waiting to pounce,
And leave the frail buds all ruthlessly torn.
Love, now an arrow piercing the body,
Friendship transformed into conscience's charity,
Life, like a sea of fog, everything dimmed,
Ideals just beckon to greater catastrophe –
Put down the wine-cup! Do not drink again, friend!
Trust in the future! Just as you trust in me.
Blow on your heart's still-glowing ember
And let us await the burning hour's clamour!
Put down the wine-cup, friend, do not drink again,
That beloved song – do you still remember:
'Ideals are the winds that fan life forever –
Happiness? No, it is not Fate's messenger.'

from *Grass on the Plain* No. 2, p. 6.

NO, YOU DID NOT DIE
Li Jiahua
dedicated to the valiant 5th April 1976

Why do you cover your face and cry   Tiananmen Square
Why do your pale lips tremble   Tiananmen Square
Why, but why, does blood run from your
    chest   Tiananmen Square
Why is your body writhing in convulsions Tiananmen Square
Reply to me   Tiananmen Square
with the burning torches and molten lava buried in your chest
With the roar and rage with which you once shook the
    universe
Surely you couldn't really die as quietly as this
surely you couldn't lose your vengeful eyes for ever after
No, you could not die
you are not dead
all the world has seen the violent anger in your features –
even in the face of stabbing knives and rifle butts
you were not afraid
unarmed the wild beast did trample over and persecute you
you would rather die than submit
valiantly lying there in the blood and tears
No, you are not dead
you can't die
your flags certainly did not fall to the ground and give up
your shredded slogan banners did not drop their flaming red
    wings
your strangled throat still continues to produce the deep roar
    of your ballads and essays as before
your mighty cannonball-fist continues spurring on and
    encouraging the battle as before
your nebulous bodily frame continues making accusations and
    calls to arms as before
Death does not belong to you
you are invincible
Yes

I believe freedom cannnot be put to death
true reason's lips cannot be sealed
then will be a day
when you will rise from the blood and tears
you will be ten, a hundred, nay one thousand times stronger
    than you are today
you will raise high anew the banner of awakening
overcoming those who before dealt with you with weapons
to solemnly proclaim out loud the rights of men.

8 April 1976
from *Enlightenment* (Guiyang branch in Beijing) No. 1, p. 21

Notes

At the turn of the year, eight people who were members of what they claimed was a nation-wide Enlightenment Society with branches in Canton, Shanghai and Guiyang, came to Beijing from Guiyang, the capital of Guizhou province. Their stated aim was to establish a Beijing branch of the Enlightenment Society, as well as to distribute their literature. A Beijing branch was established, but it soon split into two, one faction emphasizing political reform, the other stressing a revolution in culture (but not of the 1966 variety). Moreover, while in Beijing the original eight from Guiyang split, with two members breaking away to form 'Thaw' whose programme argued for a greater degree of political revolution.

The poem presented here is taken from the first magazine published by the Guiyang branch of Enlightenment in Beijing, before any internal problems arose. Like all their publications, its contents were originally published as a wall-poster first in Guiyang, then later in Beijing. The title of the whole magazine is 'The Fire God's Symphonic Poem', and it was written by Li Jiahua, who later broke away to found 'Thaw'. According to the author this poem was written three days after the Tiananmen Incident and like many other poems to have emerged in the Democracy Movement refers back to that day and its lessons.

PIONEERS
Chen Bonian

Part 1: *Parade Ground Feelings*

Wuchang parade ground is the spot where the first shots of the Wuchang Uprising were fired. In the square stands a bronze statue of Sun Zhongshan. One day in the summer of 1976 I was standing beside this statue ...

Beside the Red Building, with back to Snake Mountain,
Whose shoulders bear the endless clouds above;
Who's that standing on the parade ground,
Hat off and walking-stick pointing at the ground.

So stern his gaze
Full of the grief and suffering of the nation.
So warm his manner,
He truly is one with the people.

Ah, it is he, pioneer of China's democratic revolution,
– Great fighter, Sun Yat-sen;
Standing in the distance of time,
Scanning history, a flood of feeling like the waters of the mighty Yangtze.

That year when the signal for the Wuchang Uprising sounded,
The Yangtze River was immersed in the flying smoke of battle,
The Hall of Great Harmony was like withered leaves trembling in a fierce wind.
The fallen timbers of the decaying court crumbled away.

Ah, could a new era be dawning?
Three thousand years of darkness gone, never to return.
It is as though this senile and sickly China
Is about to shake itself and change into a handsome youth.

This is all a mere glint of golden light,
You have yet to smash the rusty shackles,
The road ahead is still so long, so long,
You have only penetrated the first mountain pass.

Look, the smoke of gunpowder where Ye Ting's Iron Army
    have taken Ding Si Bridge,
Listen, the battle cries of the heroes as they fight to open a
    road below Jinggangshan.
A forest of arms in land reform raised against tyrants.
– So far and distant is the long road against feudalism!

You are only a judgement on the decaying times,
You have no strength to deal with the tyrants one by one.
How weak is your class!
How can you use an iron fist in dealing with dukes and
princes.

You see, history sometimes has its moments
Allowing a single tyrant to push open the doors of the
    Imperial Palace bound with spider's webs.
From Yuan Shikai's ceremonial crown to Lin Biao's intrigue,
How many have conjured up dreams of gold crowns and jade
    tablets!

Oh, with face to the autumn wind, and heart burning with
    indignation and anger,
In the dead of night, face streaming with leaden tears;
If only this hand could take this staff,
And change it into a fine sharp-edged sword.

Do we stand beside you?
No, we don't stand at your side.
The great distant goals of the advancing proletariat
Have already far, far outdistanced the range of your vision.

August 1976

Part 2: *Stroll by the Red Pavilion*

Distant the great road, lofty the Red Pavilion,
The spring breeze dyes the roadside branches green once
    more.
While walking down May 4th Street
It seems I see you – Li Dazhao.

Whiskers framing your broad cheeks,
Lips breaking into a candid smile.
Through glasses perched on your nose
Your eyes flash wisdom and humanity.

Listen, how the spring wind stirs the branches,
Like your pen as it scratches across the page.
Clutching a volume of 'New Youth', leaning on a table you
    stand,
And into the morning sunlight beyond your window,
    announce a new world.

Joyfully you acclaim 'The Victory of the Masses' in the
    distance,
Predicting the world of the Red Flag planted in the bright
    dawn.
How sharp your fighting pen,
As cannon sounding on the Neva River!

Thus do you use your intellect and blood,
Fashioning arms for slaves in rebellion.
Thus do you use your red heart,
To light a lamp that shines out against the darkness of the
    past.

Your words have overcome the sharpest of barbs.
And pierced the schemes of all swindling devils.
They feared you, tracked you down,
And cast you into the lonely gloom of prison.

When you stepped up boldly to the gallows,
The storm of worker's movements was raging everywhere.
Smile indeed, who could imagine that a strip of rope could
    hold back
The surging tide of history.

You, great forerunner of revolutionary thought,
Your voice has already become the angry roar of the workers.
It reverberates still along the road of May 4th
Stirring up wave after wave in the depths of our hearts.

April 1978

from *Fertile Land* No. 1, p. 17.

Notes

An important aspect of the Democracy Movement has been the
search for respectable antecedents, and symbols which identify it
with China's revolutionary past. This poem is clearly part of that
search. Part 1 centres on the 1911 Revolution, which toppled the
Empire, and Sun Yatsen, the founder of the Chinese Republic. Part
2 focuses on Li Dazhao, a major figure in the 'May 4th Movement',
and a founder of the Chinese Communist Party. Li was librarian at
Beijing University where he had been an editor of 'New Youth', had
organized early Marxist study groups (one explanation for the
designation of the library as the 'Red' Pavilion), and where he had
written praising the Bolshevik Revolution in Russia as 'The victory
of the masses'. At the time Beijing University was on a site in the city
centre, on a street more recently named 'May 4th Street'. Much of
this poem is unoriginal. In particular, lines, verses and images in
Part 2 are heavily based on a biographical epic written by Can Kejia
and published in 1959 entitled '*Li Dazhao*' (Writers Publishing
House, Beijing). Chapters 3-5 (pages 21-31) deal with firstly, 'The
Red Pavilian – red tiles set in red light'; secondly, 'The Bolshevik
Victory'; and finally, 'May 4th – the sound of spring thunder'.

ADVICE TO CADRES

1

When ideas about work contradict, find truth by working together;

Discuss each problem in a friendly way, have mutual respect for the other;

Be considerate and modest with all whom you meet, make sure you know yourself well;

Trivia can be just brushed aside, but with matters of principle, be careful;

Self-criticism's most important, practice will show what's right;

Solve problems by revealing contradictions, not by cooling the fight;

No need to beat about the bush, it's good to be frank all the time;

Provide wisdom in leading the masses, democratic-centralism's fine;

Take no offence from differing opinions, nor attack personally;

Let's march forward together, give to the cause devotedly.

2

Be concerned with party and masses, and with yourself much less;

Thinking of others is better, encourage selflessness;

Do not intrigue against others, be open, be honourable;

Don't strive for fame, fortune, power, but only for the people;

Be helpful not wary of others, having suspicions's not right;

Each from his heart should be honest, always come straight to the point.

c

3

Lead the masses to be of one heart, appoint only capable men;
Arouse their creativity, at all costs don't inhibit them;
Don't engage in departmentalism, the spirit of cooperation's right;
Be forever tolerant, with those who differ, unite;
Change those with negative attitudes so then they'll work with a will;
Be first to bear the heaviest burdens, develop a good working-style;
Keep the masses' viewpoint always in mind, and remember to be their good pupil;
Leaderships should be revolutionized to set an example in unity;
Everyone should feel at ease with the world to work to their fullest capacity.

4

Marxism-Leninism guides us, unity's our trump card;
Never engage in factionalism, against capitalist revolutionism take guard;
Don't ever scheme or conspire, be always open and above board;
Firmly remember the 'Three Do's and Dont's', follow the revolutionary road;
Class struggle removes the scales from one's eyes, be vigilant eternally;
Be watchful for enemies who come to make trouble and splits secretly;
As one the whole nation laughs at its mantis-like enemies;
Spring has just come to our country, we'll achieve still greater victories;
Realize the 'Four Modernizations', in this beautiful country of ours.

1972

from *Masses Reference News* No. 2, p. 3.

Notes

'Masses Reference News' was largely a one-man operation. organized by Xia Shunjian, an unemployed science graduate living on the Beijing University campus. Between December 1978 and April 1979 he produced six issues of his newspaper. He was arrested on April 30th and sent back to his home town in Hunan province. It takes its title from the restricted circulation daily 'Reference News', which reproduces translated foreign language news items.

Like many of the poems to have emerged in the unofficial press this one claims to have been written before 1976 and the fall of the 'Gang of Four'. Usually this is done at least partially to prove the author's revolutionary credentials. However, this is clearly not the case here. Almost the whole poem is composed with the rhetoric and slogans in current use under the 'Gang of Four'. The exception is the last two lines which have clearly been added somewhat later referring as they do to the 'Four Modernizations'.

A POEM FOR OCTOBER
Meng Ke

Crops

Autumn steals across my face
And I am ripe.

Labour

I shall go with all the wagons,
Drawing the sunshine to the wheatfields ...

Fruit

What lovely children
A lovely sight
The red apple of the sun
And beneath it the marvellous dreams of countless children.

Autumn Wood

Not your eyes' light,
Nor your voice's sound,
Red scarves fallen on the ground ...

Encounter

A woman's silhouette
Like a cloud, floating.

The Path
That white poplar swaying unceasingly,
That girl leaning against the poplar,
That crooked road which makes the girl lose hope ...

Wind
I long to say to you:
Let us go side by side.

Clouds
I love you
When you wear that white nightgown ...

Rivers
Weary people,
You may let me clasp that wan hand.

Wife
I shall take all my days
And give them all to you.

Earth
Across all my feelings
The sun has shone.

The Bath
Stark-naked child
A woman's uncovered breast ...

Chimes
Men
Bringing warmth to the women from the midst of the
   sunshine ...

The Reclaimer
I am rivers,
I am milk,
I want to irrigate,
I want to feed,
I am an iron plough,
I am a sickle,
I want to cultivate,
I want to gather in the harvest.

Sunset
The sun moves towards the peopleless place ...

The Child
That black night approaching me says:
You are mine ...

Sleeping in the Open
Sitting face to face,
Silent face to face,
All around shack and hearth,
Men's legs, the smell of earth.

Wine
That is a lonely little grave ...

In the Fields
There, written on her solitary grave:
I have not left you anything,
I have not left myself ...

Life
Ah,
Suffering and joy already prepared for you!

Streetlamp
Even light,
Even night.

Recollection
Ah, you,
This rainbow night,
I know not how you can thus torment me.

Feeling
Startled awake,
Then fall back in love with loneliness.

Youth
Here,
In this place for greenness and growing,
I have been cast aside.

Years
Since life approached me,
She has never left.

The Poet
Put on your own heart!

Daybreak
But let you and I be of one heart,
And sweep clean the road's dark.

Baiyangdian Lake
Do not forget,
The time of joy
Will let all the fishing boats clink glasses together.

Sailboat
When that time comes,
I shall return with the windstorm.

Love
Though you are far, far from me,
I still shall be remembering:
What is mine
What you gave, all, to me.

Last Will
No matter what my name,
I hope
To leave it on this beloved ground.

Choice
Best
In waste ground
To set my life down.
Then
Welcome all seeds
To come to my fields.

Written in 1974

from *Today* No. 2, p. 1.

THE DEMOCRACY MOVEMENT55

References

[1] 'The Tiananmen Poems', Edited and Translated by Xiao Lan, Foreign Languages Press, Beijing, 1979, p. 29-30.

[2] 'The truth about the Tiananmen Incident' in *Peking Review* No. 48 (1978), 1 December 1978, p. 6ff.

[3] *Peking Review* No. 15 (1976), op. cit.

[4] The classic work on this period is Chow Tse-tsung's *The May Fourth Movement* (Harvard University Press, 1960).

[5] Xiao Lan, op. cit., p. 5. An unofficial comment along similar lines can be found in 'Enlightenment' (Guiyang Branch in Beijing) No. 1, p. 1.

[6] RMRB 16 November 1978, p. 1.

[7] See for example: '"*Siwu*" *yundong yu shehuizhuyi minzhu*' by Xu Chingwen in *Shehui Kexue zhanxian* ('Social Science's Frontline') No. 5, 20 February 1979, p. 109. The first *official* uses of the phrase '*siwu*' *yundong* (April 5th Movement) appeared in the national press on 21st November 1978.

[8] *Peking Review* No. 48 (1978) op. cit., p. 17.

[9] For example, Han Zhixiong, one of the new 'heroes' of Tiananmen, who had been arrested on April 4th, and later became a member of the Communist Youth League's Central Committee.

[10] See for example article on the Beijing Normal College in 'The Spring of Peking' No. 3, p. 16.

[11] *Peking Review* No. 4 (1978), op. cit.

[12] See for example: *Renmin jiaoyu* ('People's Education') No. 12 (1978) p. 12 'Qinghua University during the Tiananmen Incident', where Zhou Weimin, a founder of 'The Spring of Peking' is publicized.

[13] See p. 159.

CHAPTER THREE

November–December 1978: Democracy Wall and the Reversal of Verdicts

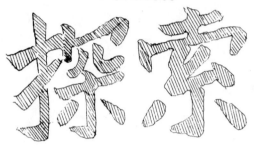

Cover of 'Exploration' No. 1, December 1978

TIANANMEN REVISITED

In retrospect, the unofficial magazine 'Science, Democracy, and Law' (which is the 'Reader's Digest' of Democracy Wall) has described the last two months of 1978 as 'The Golden Age of Democracy Wall'.[1] It is not hard to see why. Not only is it the period which saw the birth of the Democracy Movement and Democracy Wall, but all government and leadership reactions seemed at the very least to be mildly favourable. Indeed, far from opposition, most of the Democracy Movement activists seemed convinced, however naively, that they had a high degree of official support. Thus, for example, the Enlightenment Society not only took their name from a *People's Daily* editorial[2] but also claimed support from the two national daily newspapers, *People's Daily* and *Guangming Daily*.[3] Deng Xiaoping seemed to have given his support to the Democracy Movement and its activities in an interview with Robert Novak (an American journalist) on 27th November. Moreover, nigh on each and every unofficial publication justified its existence by reference to Article 45 of the Constitution, which, for example, 'April 5th Forum' reproduced immediately after its masthead on its very first edition (16th December 1978):

> Citizens enjoy freedom of speech, correspondence, the press, assembly, association, procession, demonstration and the freedom to strike ...

With hindsight the events which led to the Democracy Movement's birth have a slow-motion inevitability about them. In September 1978, there was little street political activity (mainly wall-posters and the like at that time). However, in October posters appeared on walls both in Beijing's main shopping street (Wangfu Jing) and at Xidan attacking Wu De, the Mayor of Beijing, unpopular not least because of his ostentatious involvement in the Tiananmen Incident of April 1976. (It was he who had directed the crowd to disperse over the square's loudspeaker system). Strangely enough, this was nothing new, for Wu De had been the target of wall-poster attacks intermittently for a number of years even before 1976. The crucial difference between these and previous attacks was the change in the general political environment. During the two years after October 1976 there had to all intents and purposes been a Counter Cultural Revolution. Most of those who had been publicly criticized and removed from office during the GPCR had now been rehabilitated, sometimes even posthumously, and many of the radical policies of the Cultural Revolution had been reversed. It was a period for questioning, re-examining China's recent past in order to determine, or at least attempt to plan, the future. By October 1978 few of the Cultural Revolution's radical decisions had not been reversed. Thus, Deng Xiaoping, who had been removed from office for the second time in 1976 after the Tiananmen Incident had returned to power in 1977. The only outstanding radical verdicts of the Cultural Revolution concerned the Tiananmen Incident of 1976, and the fate of several of the GPCR's 'Top Capitalist-Roaders', such as Liu Shaoqi, Peng Zhen (the former Mayor of Beijing), Tao Zhu (the pre-GPCR Central-South Regional leader), and Peng Dehuai (the Minister of National Defence until 1959 when he had clashed with Mao over development). However, any change in the official attitude towards the Tiananmen Incident was difficult while Wu De remained Mayor of Beijing. Sometime at the end of October, beginning of November, Wu Du ceased to be Mayor although he was clearly not in total (nor necessarily partial) disgrace, for he remained a member of the Politburo. His replacement as Mayor was Lin Hujia, the Mayor of Tianjin, who was not only popularly welcomed,[4] but as the poem on page 65 demonstrates, associated in the popular mind with Deng Xiaoping as another 'hero'.

On 9th November, an article appeared in the *People's Daily* which paved the way for the momentous Beijing Provincial Party Committee's decision of 15th November on the Tiananmen Incident. The first article, 'Further emancipate our minds', argued that in order to achieve the 'Four Modernizations' it was necessary to free one's mind from its previous shackles; that Mao Thought demanded that one proceeded from the actual situation, and that Mao himself was never 'shackled by any conventions'. It pointed out that 'Some comrades' thinking was still fettered by the invisible "spiritual shackles" of Lin Biao and the "Gang of Four".'[5] The stage was suitably set and on 15th November, the Tiananmen Incident was re-evaluated as a 'completely revolutionary event'.

THE BIRTH OF THE DEMOCRACY MOVEMENT

Naturally enough this re-evaluation alone may have been a necessary condition for the birth of the Democracy Movement, but it was by no means a sufficient one. It was the reactions to this decision by both the official and unofficial political systems which created the Democracy Movement. The first unofficial reactions to the Beijing Party Committee's decision were predictable enough. If the verdict on the Tiananmen Incident could be reversed, why shouldn't other decisions or attitudes be questioned? Thus, on the 16th November an anonymous poster-writer (while congratulating the Party Committee for its decision the previous day) pointed out that:

> ... Beijing citizens, who still remember Wu De's speech defining the Tiananmen riot as a counter-revolutionary political incident, are wondering why he still retains his post as a Politburo member.

Other wall-posters followed questioning the roles of individual leaders in the Cultural Revolution, as for example the simple four-liner which appeared in Tiananmen Square:

> Tao Zhu should be exonerated
> Peng Dehuai's merits greatly outweighed his errors
> Xie Fuzhi's body should be whipped 300 times
> Kang Sheng will stink forever.[6]

Even indirect attacks on Mao appeared in wall-posters. Then, on 19th November the first poster attacking Mao by name appeared. Ostensibly about Song Fuxian's play about a Shanghai family at the time of the Tiananmen Incident[7], it accused Mao of having supported the 'Gang of Four' against Deng Xiaoping, 'the representative of the Chinese proletariat'. It not only attracted large crowds but was followed by a veritable epidemic of posters, in Tiananmen Square, along Wangfu Jing, at Xidan and even in Beijing's suburbs. On the whole, these were of two types: those which defended the leadership and those which made a distinction between the 'goodies' (Deng Xiaoping, Zhao Ziyang, Wan Li, Hu Yaobang, and Lin Hujia) and the 'baddies' (Wu De, Wang Dongxing and 'other followers of the "Gang of Four"').

Official reaction to the Beijing Party Committee's decision of 15th November was slow to arrive. Indeed, the CCP's Central Committee did not give its approval until 7th December[8]. However, in the meantime 'The truth about the Tiananmen Incident' was published in almost every national newspaper on 21st November, and with it the April 5th Movement became 'officialized'. Not only had the previous verdict on the Tiananmen Incident been reversed, but it had been done in such a way as to suggest that mass activity of that kind and 'people power' no matter what, were now acceptable. Such feelings were reinforced by the publicity given to an article from the newly resurrected monthly magazine of the China Youth League entitled 'It is necessary to bring democracy into full play and consolidate the legal system' which was reprinted in the national press[9]; and an article from 'China Youth News' (of 21st November), 'The Great April 5th movement', both of which suggested that democracy had not existed during the Cultural Revolution, that people's rights had been denied and that what was required was an effective legal system and popular participation. Moreover, on the following day (22nd November) the Beijing Home Service broadcast a documentary, with on-the-spot recordings, about the Tiananmen Incident of 1976. It was entitled 'The people roar in anger – a documentary of history' and dedicated to the great Chinese people[10].

Downtown Beijing, particularly the wall at Xidan and Tiananmen Square, attracted huge crowds over the following days (25th-27th November), to read, write and discuss the many and varied posters which appeared. Naturally enough, Chinese-speaking foreigners mixed freely with the thousands at the Wall and in Tiananmen Square. Thus, on the evening of 26th November, several thousand people were gathered at the Xidan wall, after having marched in procession from Tiananmen Square (about half-a-mile) chanting 'Chinese democracy! Long live democracy!' Japanese journalists were questioned about the Chinese leadership's attitude to the current wall-posters and applause greeted their response that Deng had described Mao as too seriously ill at the end of his life to make reasonable political judgements[11]. It then transpired that there was an American journalist, Robert Novak, in the crowd due to meet Deng, and he was asked by the crowd to seek Deng's views on the Democracy Movement. He consented and promised to report back via a friend the next evening at seven o'clock. Not surprisingly, there was a large crowd present the next night. It was reported that Deng had approved of the Democracy Wall, but that he felt some of the statements made in wall-posters were incorrect. For example, he suggested that Mao was not all bad but 70% good and only 30% bad. Deng considered himself 60% good and 40% bad, percentages which he was reported as having said could be applied to Peng Dehuai, whose rehabilitation was also possible.

Those two days, November 26th and 27th, were then the turning point in the establishment of the Democracy Movement. Not only were there mass meetings in Tiananmen Square and at the newly-named Democracy Wall, not only had the Democracy Movement seemed to have gained Deng Xiaoping's seal of approval, but they were also the days when the first unofficial publications appeared. The Enlightenment Society arrived in Beijing from Guiyang (the provincial capital of Guizhou) with mimeographed copies of their wall-posters[12]; and the 'April 5th Study Group' proposed the creation of an alternative press[13]. There can be little doubt that the

Democracy Movement activists felt that they were not only acting within the law, but also being encouraged to air their views. Thus, most of the unofficial publications justified their existence not only within the rights of the Constitution but also sometimes by reference to the current leadership and even Mao Zedong. [The initial statement of 'April 5th', 'Exploration', 'The Spring of Peking' and 'Today' are provided in Appendix Two.] The first issue of the 'April 5th Forum' even went so far as to suggest that the relationship between the official and unofficial press would have dialectically pleased Mao Zedong[14].

However, what appeared on Democracy Wall and in the unofficial press for what remained of November and the whole of December was in the main part very cautious, dealing with the immediate (such as Democracy Wall itself) and with well tried themes. Thus, Li Hongkuan's extremely anodyne 'Odes to Democracy and the Constitution' are representative of a substantial part of the Democracy Movement's output at the time. Even more popular themes were those which attacked the 'Gang of Four', or which sought the reversal of verdicts on past events or individual politicians. In particular there seems to have been a groundswell of support for the rehabilitation of Peng Zhen, the former Mayor of Beijing. A wish that was granted in January, for at the turn of the year almost all the remaining 'Top Capitalist Roaders' of GPCR, with the exception of Liu Shaoqi were rehabilitated, following the Third Plenum of the 11th Central Committee[15].

There were, however, three new developments in the Democracy Movement during December which were to play a substantial role later on. The first was the publication of Wei Jingsheng's posters (later produced as 'Exploration' No. 1) on 'The Fifth Modernization – Democracy'. The second was the emergence of a 'human rights' section within the Democracy Movement. Two open letters were posted as wall-posters – the first to Carter on December 10th and the second to Brzezinski on December 15th. Both told very much the same story. To quote from the latter, by a Beijing Construction worker:

> Human rights in China have suffered the most terrible
> attacks and are still totally denied ... The ghost of human
> rights will haunt China forever ... Throughout China, there
> are cases of wrongful persecution, injustice, hunger, and
> forced separation of families ... We hope that you and
> President Carter will be even more concerned with the
> human rights movement in our country in the future ...[16]

Finally, there was the start of a trend against both Deng
Xiaoping and his policy of rapid modernization, because he
was thought to be too defensive of Mao; and not aware enough
of the dangers inherent in modernization, namely the possible
appearance in China of a privileged class of bureaucrats as in
the USSR. As one anonymous writer wrote in early
December:

> What kind of modernization does China plan to achieve?
> The Soviet, American, Japanese, or Yugoslav type? We the
> ordinary masses know nothing of these issues ... I work
> hard, even exceeeding my quotas, but after my shift I just
> like to ponder what I have been working for ...

To which a reader had written in reply:

> Deng should come here and read these wall-posters instead
> of apologizing for Chairman Mao's mistakes.

PLEASE FOLLOW BIG MAN DENG
– to Lin Hujia

One
Quickly settle the waters of Tianjin.
The bright Milky Way became soaking rain,
Who would have thought there were no clouds in Beijing?
Please quickly settle the waters of Tianjin,
Don't disappoint the long-standing wishes of the masses.

Two
Follow Big Man Deng.
Changan's elders await your presence,
Please follow Big Man Deng.
Mend bones, disperse poison, remove boils,
Let a wave of goodness save the key link.

Three

A body with a hundred sicknesses can live

The ones who come to see doctors day and night have tracks of
    tears,

Suddenly one meets a god who raises the dead.

With my whole body I trust these words:

A miracle can let a body with a hundred sicknesses live.

Four

Flowers bloom, willows green, spring is on the shore.

Lin bends in the greenery and grows new trees himself,

He chops off the poisonous stems of sick trees.

Then you can recognize all seedlings and waving grasses,

By themselves flowers bloom, willows green, spring is on the
    shore.

Praise Lin Hujia.

Riding a running horse, holding a sword he smashed the
    shackles,

Then bending he shoots a lethargic crow.

Thunder resounds with marching drums,

He dares to subjugate the flowers in the backyard of the
    nation.

from Science, Democracy and Law No. 1, p. 7.

Notes

In October 1978, Wu De the Mayor of Beijing was replaced by Lin
Hujia. Wu had been Mayor at the time of the Tiananmen Incident
and had broadcast a message asking the crowd to disperse on the
evening of April 5th 1976. His replacement as Mayor was
presumably linked to the decision to reverse the verdict on the
Tiananmen Incident, although Wu himself retained his Politburo
membership. Prior to his appointment in Beijing, Lin Hujia had
been the popular Mayor of Tianjin, where in addition to
reorganizing the city in the wake of the 1976 earthquake, he had
become famous for his irrigation construction. In this poem he is
being urged to emulate the also popular Deng Xiaoping. 'Big Man'
Deng is presumably a play on both his name (Xiaoping means 'little
peace' in Chinese) and diminutive size.

ODE TO 'DEMOCRACY WALL'

A white stone brick wall at Xidan,
calmly stands by Changan Street.
Accompanied by chimes from the Telegraph Building,
it closely watches people's trends.
Even if you are not grand and imposing,
nor magnificent and beautiful,
you're extremely ordinary, ordinary.

In the China of the Seventies,
you send out the calls of the times!
The cry of a new arrival
echoes all around, forcefully.
'We want democracy!'
'We want science!'
'We want a legal system!'
'We want the Four Modernizations!'

These cries already old, pressed on people's chests,
these desires buried for years in people's hearts!
People hail them.
Because you,
express people's ideals.
Here
one can finally breathe the air of freedom,
Here
one can finally feel the power of the masses.

Some are astounded, frightened.
Traditional ignorance still binds their thoughts.
Here they carefully inspect the new world.
Sometimes they close their eyes for fear,
but don't see the itch in their hearts.

Some are in a fury, panic.
You are a sharp sword,
Ruthlessly you stab at demons and monsters.
You burn the raging flames of revolution,
glistening with the radiance of truth.

You are a mirror to the society of China,
impartially reflect the appearance of society.
All hideous things are revealed,
all beautiful things receive praise.

People with grievances come here to tell,
at pains come and talk before you,
People with opinions put them to you
unconcernedly they can present their ideas on governing as
                                                    well.
Here the darkness of society is exposed,
Here the livers of Lin Biao and the Gang of Four are dissected.
Here the robe of religion is cast off;
Here the throne of despotism is set on fire;
Immortals smashed images of emperors and kings!

The soldiers of the Paris Commune
falling held on to the 'Wall of the Commune',
the already awakened Chinese giant
in his blood writes
compositions about communes on 'Democracy Wall'.

Although blue ghosts wander amongst the masses,
and the sound of handcuffs resounds in people's ears;
Although closed chains already smothered countless lives,
the claws of Fascism again stretched out to burning chests.
The people did not yield,
in the high song of freedom of Democracy Wall.

Cry out! – Democracy Wall,
the trend of the times is gathering in front of you,
rolling forward! No man can stop it!
Fight! – Democracy Wall.
People stand in front of you arm in arm,
to fight for a lofty ideal,
fearless against blood-stained weapons!
I praise you Democracy Wall,
you symbolize the light of China,
stand for man's hopes,
Forever you will be in people's hearts,
imprinted in the nation's glorious history!

from *The Spring of Peking* No. 2, p. 2.

Notes

As the Democracy Movement has developed, so Democracy Wall itself has become a symbol for the movement. At the same time the nascent movement has still sensed a need to present its credentials in terms of other movements, symbols and slogans. Thus in this poem, the slogans of the May 4th Movement for Science and Democracy are combined with the new calls for an effective legal system and the 'Four Modernizations'; agriculture, industry, science and technology. Again there is reference to the Paris Commune, and against Lin Biao and the 'Gang of Four'.

DAWN
A Peking Worker

Walking out in a very thick fog
I lose my way. Where am I heading?
Wondering if there's still a sun in the world
As I went through the fog, I was shouting –
Brothers and Sisters
All dear to me! Where are you?
All of a sudden a shaft of sunlight
Strikes through the fog – oh so precious.
Towards it I'm running, I'm flying.
Ahead, brothers and sisters, younger sisters too are coming.
China is the native place of Mao Zedong Thought.
Let's go forward hand in hand,
March forward towards the bright dawning.
The early morning sunlight chases the fog away,
On 'Democracy Wall'
The People have shown their strength.

7th December.

from *April 5th Forum* No. 2, p. 3.

ODES TO DEMOCRACY AND THE CONSTITUTION
Li Hongkuan

To Democracy

The clouds melt and the mists disperse as the heart's shutter
    opens.
Socialist Democracy is like a bud.
A thousand armies and ten thousand horses hasten the Four
    Modernizations.
Long live the spirit of April 5th.
Democracy and Law established at the heroes' monument,
The masses know best, deeds and misdeeds.
Ideas and wisdom want to be newly set free,
The democratic constitution releases golden splendour.

To the Constitution

The 5th National People's Congress opens red flowers,
Drawing up the people's new constitution.
Eight hundred million people joyously sing together,
Of one heart to establish a new nation.

The fresh blood of the revolutionary martyrs is sprinkled,
In exchange for today's new constitution.
Protect democracy, protect people's rights,
Advance the Four Modernizations.

The strength of the masses is great,
Mount the fine horse at the great red time.
All corners of the country sing out in praise –
We have friends all over the world.

from *Science, Democracy and Law* No. 2, p. 15.

Notes

The First Session of the Fifth National People's Congress met
February-March 1978 in Beijing.

WHERE IS THE CULTURAL REVOLUTION GROUP?
Huai De

The Cultural Revolution Group has disappeared,
On a paper ship burning, a lamp lighting the sky,
All ghosts, monsters, demons, caught in one net,
The fog wrapped round the world's now lifted and gone.

Think back to those ten years of Cultural Revolution and
    chaos,
It's hard to forget such demons and the rumpus they made,
Kang Sheng, the old gangster, served as Adviser,
Group Leader was the reptilian witch Jiang Qing.

Beneath them a group of sinister pen-pushers,
And the army as well commanded by Lin Biao,
Together they seized party, state, and military power,
While the Big Five Guards went along for the fun.

In plotting a coup d'état, Lin Biao died early,
Although Kang Sheng died, people can't forgive him,
Jiang, Wang, Yao, and Zhang were finally arrested,
When we like we can punish the Big Five Red Guards.

He who moves a heavy boulder easily crushes his own feet,
And one at a time they expended themselves,
As before our country's redder than red,
For the pests are all gone to meet what they deserve.

from *The Spring of Peking* No. 1, p. 34.

Notes

This poem is directed against the coalition of forces that helped
Mao launch the Cultural Revolution. The Cultural Revolution
Group was that established by the Party centre in 1966 in order to
oversee the Great Proletarian Cultural Revolution. Its Director was
Mao's wife, Jiang Qing, and Kang Sheng, a favourite target of
attack for the Democracy Movement, was attached to the Group as
Adviser. Lin Biao was the Minister of National Defence and Mao's
chosen successor during the Cultural Revolution until his death in
1971. He was later accused of having plotted a coup d'état. The Big
Five Red Guards were the leaders of the Red Guard movement in

Beijing during the Great Proletarian Cultural Revolution. Despite
the implication in the poem that all five were still alive, in fact one,
Wang Dabin of the Geological Institute was killed in 1970. Jiang
(Qing), Wang (Hongwen), Yao (Wenyuan), and Zhang
(Chunqiao) were the 'Gang of Four'.

THE VOICE OF THE PEOPLE
Zheng Ming

– straight from the heart –

What precisely was the nature of Liu Shaoqi's crimes,
And when will we hear *his* side of the story.
When we do it's certain that his criminal reputation
Will sink in a sea of false accusations and never be heard of
    again:

      for Liu Shaoqi was not guilty!

Peng Dehuai was a man of great merit,
Who embraced virtue and gave his all for China.
Who knows what injustices he suffered,
For he was accused without substance:

      indeed Peng Dehuai was falsely accused!

Ho 'The Dragon' 's battles did him great credit,
For when the dragon rose he fought heroically.
How was his contribution wiped from the slate,
When everyone knew his high reputation,

      since Ho Long's achievements were great!

Old Commander Chen was as dependable as the oldest
    mountains.
A solid piece of white jade without a single flaw, like virgin
    snow.
A shining example, honest and open-minded,
He was China's great warrior-hero:

      and Chen Yi was honourable!

The difficulties put in Tao Zhu's path and his removal from
    office,
Amount to a gross error for he was a pillar of the state.
When will his good name be restored,
And the accusations against him removed?

      for what, if any, were Tao Zhu's crimes?

Peng Zhen was a good mayor,
Always on hand when needed, he was truly able.
Then was Peking's 'Golden Age',
So when is he going to return to office:

      where are you now Peng Zhen?

Thus in the past there've been serious injustices,
And these comrades were severely persecuted.
But nowadays everyone's angry,
And wants to change that state of affairs.

Come quickly friends and comrades!
Unlike before, we've no doubts now!
Shake off the chains which bind you,
And demand that blood debts be honoured.

                from *The Spring of Peking* (5 March 1979), p. 34.
Notes

This poem, like many of the wall-posters of the Democracy
Movement, asks for a 'redress of grievances' on behalf of, and the
'reversal of verdicts' on six top leaders from before 1966, who were
criticized during the Great Proletarian Cultural Revolution. All but
Liu Shaoqi have in fact now been fully 'rehabilitated', and although
Liu still awaits posthumous re-recognition, his name is no longer
besmirched as it once was. Moreover, his widow, Wang Guangmei,
who was 'purged' at the same time, was rehabilitated in January
1979. On the other hand, all but Peng Zhen are now dead. Peng
Dehuai and Tao Zhu were officially (and posthumously)
rehabilitated in December 1978, and Peng Zhen at the end of
January 1979.

    Two interesting aspects of this poem are its uses of the pun and
the 'hidden line'. First, the content of each of the six verses referring

to specific leaders is in fact a play on the meaning of that leader's name. Thus the verse on Peng Zhen plays on the meaning of *zhen* as real or true; that on Chen Yi focuses on *yi* as firm, steadfast, dependable, resolute, etc.; that on Peng Dehuai, makes play with *de* meaning virtue. For this reason alone, Ho Long has been referred to as Ho 'The Dragon'.

Second, this poem is written in such a way in Chinese that each of the first six verses (those referring to specific leaders) is not only four lines of six characters when read from left to right, but there is also a fifth line of four characters when the first character in each line is read from top to bottom. For these six verses, this fifth line has been translated as a final chorus. (See endpiece)

The author of this poem signs himself Zheng Ming. This is clearly a pseudonym, as *zheng ming* means 'struggle to air one's opinion'.

CHERISH THE MEMORY OF PENG ZHEN

The people of Peking,
For Peng Zhen fondly yearn.
Where are you now?
Of you there's been no word or sound.
Even in the dark and gloomy past,
Your promise was still around.
So night and day we long for you in office,
And that you'll soon return.

from Science, Democracy and Law No. 1, p. 1.

Selections from

AN ETERNITY OF DEEDS AND MISDEEDS
Tai Chi

Prologue

For thousands of miles rivers and mountains sang bitter tears,
For four thousand days the world was turned upside down.
The nightmare dragged on too long.
Deeds, good or bad, who's to say?

No need to appeal to god or emperor,
Our bleeding hearts will tell the truth.
Don't approach the scholar or genius,
But Mount Tai and the Yellow River.

Back cover of a Red Guard Journal from the Great Proletarian Cultural Revolution attacking Peng Zhen. The cartoon is entitled 'Down with Peng Zhen!' and shows him inter alia 'for Liu Shaoqi and the bourgeoisie and against Mao: but Peng and his ilk can never match Mao and the masses'.

《怀念彭真》———— 北京人

北京人民，
怀念彭真。
你在哪里？
不见音仪。
黑暗已去，
光明来临。
日夜盼望，
早些出任。

习的女子极了，
说出首都人民的心里话！   11.29

Poem as posted on Democracy Wall – 'Cherish the memory of Peng Zhen'.

The People's mountains and rivers are real enough,
They're accustomed to rising winds and falling clouds,
Spring flowers and autumn fruits through endless generations,
They firmly believe in the laws of history:

– those who sow puncture vine
　will be torn by the thorns of the plant;
– the gardener who seeds the beauty of spring
　is entitled to harvest happiness.

The Cultural Revolution

Truth and fallacy all mixed together
Revolutionary slogans raised in one place, lowered in another.
Mass movements – where the mass was moved,
Clouds and winds never settled – the battle was a jigsaw.

The moment one bit into another's neck
His own wrists were caught from behind;
Murderers stood high on the reviewing stand.
The free and unfettered were struck by disasters as bolts from
　　the blue.

As paint pots that were broken
All colours fused together, not a one untainted.
Like looking through a kaleidoscope
Eyes were dazzled from the constant change of scenes.

Mad men ran after men half-mad
Each and every person was sucked down into the whirlpool.
When, at last the clamour ceased,
One basked in the sun, scratched one's head, and wondered
　　why.

Mao Zedong

Son of the Shaoshan plain,
Giant of the Chinese revolution.
The people praised you
The evil and crafty made you, into a god.

Demon, devil, and witch,
Blocked out our sun with fog.
It's time to peel off your godlike gloss,
And give back to the people the leader they had.

Zhou Enlai

1

You didn't leave descendants
Nor tomb or tombstone,
You didn't even leave your ashes
But scattered over the country they signalled your love for the
    people.

You were the wealthier though, by far,
The owner of eight hundred million hearts,
Our motherland has taken your ashes
And developed a Zhou Enlai spirit.

2

To build a memorial hall, or issue your collected works;
Are such things really necessary.
Mountains will never grow old and rivers always flow,
As long as the people remember.

Kang Sheng

1

Man or ghost, one really can't tell,
Half devil, half mortal, nicknamed 'incorruptible'.
Although busy, he could still act as go-between,
And even at leisure he fought with his pen.

Through *that* woman's connections he became a top
    counsellor,
He wrote vitriol everywhere and dished out the orders,
Heaped corpses like mountains, made the sea look like blood,
Content with his achievements, he carried an endless namelist
    of victims around in his pocket.

2

He was good at reading people's faces,
Prepared to fish with a long line and wait in Jiang Qing's
    service,
In troubled waters he showed his great ability,
And his hat was red because of other's blood.

It was a pity his companions didn't last so long,
And this old gangster himself vanished before his time,
Although his bones lie buried in Baobashan
We'll settle scores with him one day.

The Triumph of October

April 5th was bleeding, many people dead and dying.
But the party was still vigilant
Painfully contemplating
Waiting for October.

The 'Four Pests' were removed forever
Neatly and tidily, without a gunshot.
Everyone raised their glasses high,
Crabs were eaten and maotai drunk.

Deng Xiaoping

Wise and talented, like the Duke of Zhou, he's Hua's right
    hand.
He'll chat and laugh easily, and by lifting a finger make
    people and country happy and peaceful.
Don't be surprised that he's fallen twice and risen three times,
There are always traitors on the road to revolution.

His heart goes out to the whole country.
Because of his misfortunes he can see more clearly.
A Monkey King, who once he'd left Heaven's Gate
Became as important as the mountains, a living god.

Peng Zhen

We still remember Peng Zhen's removal
The streets overflowed with people
'Swear to Criticize Peng!'
  'Raise High the Banner of Mao Zedong's Thought!'
    'Closely Follow Mao's Instructions!'
We were all children then.

It's hard to detail the Cultural Revolution's achievements.
Now people have woken, they lick their wounds themselves.
When we happen to meet a friend in the street it's like seeing a
    ghost;
Two birds together frightened of being shot but yearning for
    the other's company.

The 3rd Plenum of the 11th Central Committee

1

History cannot be denied
The country would be insulted.
The spirit of the state's heroic founders can't be killed by its
    enemies
Why else did they leave us their legacy?

The people shout at the top of their voice
The Party's Central Committee sees far ahead
The 3rd Plenum raised the red banner high
Its characters read – Democracy!

2

Each line of the 3rd Plenum's communique is thunder
Rumbling in the depths of our hearts.
Though loud the thunder, there's been little rain
But the masses keep looking to the heavens.
Without curing the wounds of the mind
How can we advance to the 'Four Modernizations'?
The top and basic levels are enthusiastic, but the middle
    layers are not.
Wherever there is a septic boil, it should be lanced.

from *Harvest* No. 1, p. 15.

Notes

The nine poems presented here are part of a much longer 28-part work dealing with the events and personalities of China's politics from the start of the Cultural Revolution to the end of 1978. There are three sections, with the 'goodies' sandwiching the 'baddies'. The full list of contents is:

Prologue

The Cultural Revolution
Mao Zedong
Zhou Enlai
Liu Shaoqi
Zhu De
Peng Dehuai
Ho Long
Chen Yi
Tao Zhu

The April 5th Movement
Lin Biao
Kang Sheng
Chen Boda
Zhang Chunqiao
Jiang Qing
Xie Fuzhi
Yao Wenuan
Wang Hongwen

The Triumph of October
Hua Guofeng
Yed Jianying
Deng Xiaoping
Chen Yun
Peng Zhen
Hu Yaobang

The Third Plenum (of the 11th Central Committee)
Conclusion

Comments on a couple of the poems translated here are perhaps necessary. As the third anniversary of Zhou Enlai's death approached, suggestions were made in wall-posters and elsewhere that he should be afforded some sign of public recognition. One such

D

was the blueprints for a Zhou Enlai memorial, to be sited between
Mao's Mausoleum and the Revolutionary Martyrs' Memorial in
Tiananmen Square, which were posted on walls around Beijing in
December.

Kang Sheng has been a major target of attack for the Beijing
Democracy Movement. He is rumoured to be the person who
brought Mao and Jiang Qing together in Yanan, and was Adviser to
Jiang Qing's Cultural Revolution Group during the late 1960s. In
the Qing court it was the practice for high officials to wear red hats
as a mark of office.

In 1976, following the Tiananmen Incident on April 5th came
Mao's death in September, and the removal of the Gang of Four in
October. October is not only the month for eating crabs, but the
crab is the symbol of a tyrant.

Where Kang Sheng and Wang Dongxing have been the major
targets of attack for the Beijing Democracy Movement, Deng
Xiaoping and Peng Zhen have received the best press. During the
last three years Deng has clearly inherited the mantle of Zhou Enlai,
hence the ambiguity of the reference to the Duke of Zhou, the
minister of Wu Wang the first emperor of the Zhou dynasty (during
the 11th Century BC) and traditionally the model for the good
administrator. Moreover, Deng's second removal from high office as
a result of the Tiananmen Incident (the first was during the Cultural
Revolution) has served to underline this reputation. Popularly he
has become known as 'Big Man' Deng, a play on both his name and
size, and equated with the mischievous folk-hero the Monkey King,
who despite all adversities always comes out on top. Peng Zhen was
the Mayor of Beijing until the Cultural Revolution when he was
removed from office as being one of Mao's bitterest opponents. He
was rehabilitated in January 1979 amidst signs of his evident
popularity and calls for his return to office on the streets of Beijing.
Since his rehabilitation he has been Chairman of the National
People's Congress Legal Committee.

The Third Plenum of the Eleventh Central Committee of the
Chinese Communist Party was held in December 1978 in Beijing.
Apart from calling a halt to the campaign against the 'Gang of
Four', and re-emphasizing the need to achieve the 'Four
Modernizations', the Plenum also agreed to the rehabilitation of
several former leading cadres who had been attacked during the
Cultural Revolution.

References

1 'Science, Democracy and Law' No. 15, 20 June 1979, 'Forward'.
2 RMRB 22 July 1978, 'Enlightened philosophy and philosophical enlightenment'.
3 'Enlightenment' (Guiyang Branch in Beijing) No. 2, 24 November 1978, p. 3.
4 SWB FE 5968/BII/8 14 November 1978, 'Lin Hujia's concern for Beijing's People Living Problems', (New China News Agency, 11 November 1978) showed the official media 'doing their bit' to promote Lin's popularity.
5 For full text see SWB FE 5968/BII/1, 14 November 1978.
6 Xie Fuzhi and Kang Sheng were leading 'Maoists' during the GPCR. Both were Politburo members. Xie died in 1972, Kang in 1975.
7 *Yu wu sheng chu* ('Where the silence is'.) (*Shanghai wenyi chubanshe, Shanghai*, 1978).
8 SWB FE 5911/BII/11 11 December 1978, New China News Agency (NCNA) report, 7 December 1978.
9 *Zhongguo qingnian* ('China's Youth') No. 3, 1978, p. 33 in RMRB 13 November 1978.
10 SWB FE 5978/BII/3 25 November 1978.
11 SWB FE 5982/BII/2 30 November 1978; Kyodo in English, 27 November 1978.
12 See 'No, you did not die.' p. 43.
13 See Appendix 2, p. 159.
14 'April 5th Forum' No. 1, 16 December 1978, p. 1.
15 'Communique of the Third Plenary Session of the 11th Central Committee of the Communist Party of China', (adopted on 22 December 1978) in *Peking Review* No. 52, 29 December 1978, p. 13-14.
16 *Daily Telegraph* 18 December 1978.

CHAPTER FOUR

January–February 1979: Human Rights, Privileges and the Coming of Spring

北京之春

THE SPRING OF PEKING

79.1.

目　　录

Where the Democracy Movement had stumbled into existence during the last two months of 1978, in January and February 1979 it really began to take on a life of its own. Partially, this was because of the liberalizing trends in national politics, and partially because the Democracy Movement itself became more organized. Three themes dominated the Democracy Movement during these months – the question of human rights, attacks on the privileges of cadres, and a certain naive hope that the coming spring would bring radical change. It should perhaps be explained that whereas the Spring Festival (28 January in 1979) occurs during Beijing's winter it is in fact the traditional (agricultural calendar) New Year and so has many of the same connotations of 'newness' as in English.

On the whole the leadership's attitude to the Democracy Movement was very laissez-faire during January and February. Largely, this was because it had other concerns, major amongst which in January were the attempts to re-create an effective legal system (a job entrusted to the newly rehabilitated Peng Zhen),[1] and a re-examination of China's past developmental experience and Mao's role. Since these were tasks also being discussed by the Democracy Movement, the leadership would clearly have lost much of its newly gained popularity if in arguing for 'socialist democracy' it had been seen to suppress the street activists immediately. Moreover, at the time, much of the Democracy Movement's literature carried the same message as official publications – namely that democracy was necessary if the 'Four Modernizations' were to be realized. It would have been a very strange situation – though by no means impossible in China – that whilst participants in a CCP Propaganda Department Work Conference (from mid-January to mid-February) were re-assessing Mao as a 'Left-adventurist' for his policies after 1958, action was taken against those who unofficially in public were merely suggesting that Mao was after all mortal. Then in February, the leadership's main concern became the war against Vietnam.

However, this laissez-faire attitude was not repeated at all levels of authority. Towards the end of January, possibly around the 23rd, the Beijing Party Committee attempted to check the Democracy Movement somewhat. In an internal circular, handwritten purported copies of which were posted on Democracy Wall, it seemed that the Beijing authorities were prepared to be tougher than in the past:

> Wall-posters in the streets are developing a tendency to proliferate. There are all sorts, some in praise of Chairman Mao and Premier Zhou, some demand human rights, a small number have political content, and some are extremely revolutionary. This has been the case ever since the reversal of the verdict on the Tiananmen Incident ...
> A small number of them attack Chairman Mao and some people are printing underground publications. There is the 'April 5th Forum' and an 'Enlightenment Society' ...
> ... some are organizing underground organizations, some are engaged in petitioning activities. On 8th January, in the evening, some people organized a petitioners' group, handed out written material and organized another demonstration. On 14th January they organized another demonstration.

The circular then went on to criticize relations between foreigners and Chinese, claiming that foreigners were helping the Democracy Movement and implying links with Taiwan. It also appealed to citizens' civic responsibilities suggesting that 'the proliferation of wall-posters is making a mess of the city'. It finished with the salutary warnings that those who were 'counter-revolutionary' or indolent youth would be suitably punished, and that when:

> ... some Chinese accept foreigners' invitations to go to a restaurant to eat, this is a loss of honour to the country. Some people not only eat food with foreigners they even ask for things from them. This is also a loss of honour to the country.

However, the only tangible action which followed this circular was that wall-posters were cleared off the walls and buildings on Wangfu Jing – the main shopping street alongside the Beijing Hotel.

That the Democracy Movement was able to ride this storm was due not only to differences between the national and municipal authorities, but also to its own growth since mid-November. New organizations had come into being at the turn of the year (and especially in preparation for 8th January – the anniversary of Zhou Enlai's death) to join those already established – The Enlightenment Society, 'Exploration', the 'April 5th Forum', and 'Masses Reference News'. In particular, the Human Rights Alliance had been formed at the start of the year and published a 'Nineteen point Chinese Declaration of Human Rights';[2] and what were to become the two most popular unofficial publications, namely 'The Spring of Peking' and 'Today', were founded. The first, in effect, represented the 'liberal' wing of the Beijing Young Communist League, with many of its activists who were members; and the second was, undoubtedly, the most professionally-published of all the unofficial publications.

Moreover, Democracy Movement activists, and particularly those in the Human Rights Alliance, had broadened the scope of their activities, to include (amongst others) giving support to the individuals, groups and representatives from the provinces who came to the capital seeking work, food, or redressal of their 'grievances' dating from the days of the Cultural Revolution. Many had come since the late summer of 1978, and during the winter, as 'To Beijing' emphasises (p. 91) it became a serious problem. The Beijing authorities' response was to arrest Fu Yuehua (at her home on 18th January), one of the leading organizers of both the Human Rights Alliance and its aid for 'petitioners', as the out-of-towners were often called, and to issue its circular around 23rd January.

The Democracy Movement's reaction was spirited, if only partially effective. On 25th January all the various 'mass organizations' and unofficial publications, with the notable exception of 'The Spring of Peking' issued a joint statement which pledged them all 'To implement and defend Articles 45 and 52 of the Constitution' (those guaranteeing individual's rights and freedoms), 'To realize socialist democracy', and to mutual support in case of attack[3]. Representations on behalf of Fu Yuehua were indeed made but these came to nothing and she remained in the hands of the public security forces[4]. However, the Democracy Movement's unity was temporary and fragile at best, whereas the CCP's leadership was soon to become much less tolerant.

THE PREMIER'S 'MEMORIAL HALL'

Families hang the Premier's portrait on their wall,
Homes are like a 'Memorial Hall',
Eight hundred million people, eight hundred million minds,
The most glorious in all countries at all times,
In this world such blessings are only for the Supreme,
People look up daily with esteem,
Public opinion polls pass on the heart's sound
Show he's really the Red Sun we revolve around.

from *Science, Democracy and Law* No. 1, p. 10.

Notes

As the third anniversary of Zhou Enlai's death approached, suggestions appeared in wall-posters on Beijing's walls for a suitable memorial to the former premier. Towards the end of December 1978 there was a substantial debate about the need for any such memorial. This poem was a contribution to the debate. There are, as yet, no opinion pollsters in the PRC. During the GPCR Mao was referred to as the 'Red Sun'.

TO BEIJING

On winter nights
the white cold winds blow through dull and lonely streets and
    lanes.
People fall slowly.
Heaven takes those seekers for help in its care;
their souls choke back their blood-stained tears;
but their bodies still lie in the streets.
To this dawning city,
hateful eyes are torn and ripped open.
It's an old story,
but it happened here.
The date – January 1979,
the place – Beijing.

1

People
Picture yourselves in the delicate and graceful waves of a
    waltz.
Pave small streets with your tender eye.
In those small streets you meet your lover.
Picture yourselves behind a counter.
Take this month's pay from your wallet.
For a girl-friend about to marry,
you choose a fine pair of vases.
Or, against seemingly endless winter nights,
you shut tight the doors of the rooms in your house.
After that, you caress your sweet little daughter,
and sink with her into the dreamland of a rainbow.

I suppose,
you can feel content.
Content with the comfort and peace of this life.
You can enjoy this winter night deep in snow.
Can be thankful for the icicles
that pattern your glass windows with beautiful designs.

Yet you have not realized
that what you locked outside
is not only the cold of the night.
There are also people like you, suffering, appealing for help.
Amidst hunger and cold, countless brothers are struggling.
You turn your eyes away,
forget that the Gang of Four left its invisible marks on you too.
You just closed your eyes
and sank into a tranquil frame of mind.

2

A man goes begging
A woman goes begging
A child goes begging
Pairs of pairs of unhappy pleading eyes
Crowds of crowds in rags rounded the corners of the streets
holding up banners, shouting
          'Oppose hunger!'
          'Oppose cold!'

My beloved
     parents
     brothers
     sisters
even when you have been
     diligent workers
     honest peasants
     cadres
     students
if in this existence you're deprived of your rights,
you'll just have to leave it all behind.
The great door of democracy
will be forever firmly closed.
As told by glinting bayonets:
'Exercise dictatorship over the ones closed out!'

Why do you want to come here
and silently wait.
Why are you here, freezing and starving to death?
Is it possible you still think
among the spirits taken in by the Gang of Four
are those who beg for justice?
Is it possible you still think those callous hearts
bear sympathy towards another man.

My unlucky sisters
My beloved brothers
Come, let us walk arm in arm.
Let us straighten out our thoughts together.
Our hearts and yours beat in one rhythm.
Let our roar reach to the high wall of 'Democracy'.
Let us use our blood and lives
and fight for truth and justice.

Our brothers have fallen in a political incident.
Their deaths dawn on the city.
Their bodies still lie in the streets.
To Beijing hateful eyes are torn and ripped open.

Shame!
Beijing's people.
Shame!
People's Beijing.

from *The People's Forum* (20th January 1979)

Notes

'The People's Forum' was a totally one-man operation. Originally
associated with 'April 5th Forum' its author first wrote and
produced the one issue of 'The People's Forum' and then joined
'Exploration'.

In 1978 the Chinese leadership promoted the 'redressing of
grievances' suffered under the 'Gang of Four' during the decade
1966-1976. At the highest levels of the leadership this involved the
rehabilitation (sometimes even posthumously) of cadres purged
during the Cultural Revolution, and more generally the pursuit of

more populist and popular policies than in the immediate past. During the summer of 1978, individuals, groups and delegations, (particularly of peasants from the countryside) from many provinces came to Beijing to obtain redress for their grievances, to complain about their conditions, or simply looking for work. For the most part they lived out on the streets, particularly in the old legation quarter, close by the Beijing reception centre for those arriving from out of town. However, what was possible in the summer was not in the winter. At least eight of the 'seekers for help' described in this poem died of exposure during December and January from attempting to live out on the streets, and it is clearly these deaths which have prompted the author.

'THERE'S A HOUSING SHORTAGE IN BEIJING ...'
A Revolutionary Citizen

There's a housing shortage in Beijing,
But in Zhongnanhai new buildings are built.
When Chairman Mao and Premier Zhou were still alive,
Was there that kind of extavagent spending?
Sites of culture and history are completely demolished –
Really it's not just absurd but gross!
There's a forest of building cranes which daily revolve,
And the lorries are busy throughout the nights.
The seasons come and the seasons go,
Still half the city's construction force is employed here:
If local authorities thus break the law, they should be severely
    punished,
For when those above behave unworthily, those below will do
    the same.
Premier Zhou's attitude to the masses should be copied
Rather than Qin Shihuang's when he built the Afang palace.
Think carefully Vice-Chairman Wang,
We lesser mortals only live in two square metres each.

from *The Spring of Peking* No. 1, p. 33.

Notes

The main target of this poem is Wang Dongxing, Vice chairman of the CCP, and long reputed to be in charge of the Administrative

Office in Zhongnanhai, the headquarters of the Politburo and State Council, and home of all China's top leaders. Qin Shihuang was the unifier of China (221 BC), and is justifiably regarded as a tyrant, since his aim seems to have been the creation of a totalitarian state. In the 'Criticize Lin Biao, Criticize Confucius' campaigns of 1973-5, Qin Shihuang and the 'Legalists' received better notices than Confucius and his school of philosophy (of which Lin Biao was said to be a disciple). The explicit identification of Mao Zedong with Qin Shihuang made during these campaigns suggest that the reference to Qin Shihuang in this poem is hardly accidental.

CHAIRMAN'S TOMB AND EMPEROR'S PALACE
Qu Tian

Chairman's tomb and Emperor's palace
    face each other across the square,
One great leader in his wisdom
    made our countless futures bare,
Each and every marble staircase
    covers heaps of bones beneath,
From the eaves of such fine buildings
    fresh red blood drops everywhere.

from *Exploration* No. 3, p. 10.

Notes

'Exploration' was probably the most radical of all the unofficial publications produced in Beijing during the winter of 1978/9. Its most famous publication (and certainly its most influential) was originally a wall-poster entitled 'The Fifth Modernization – Democracy', whose main argument became the theme of the 'Democracy Movement', namely that China's drive for modernization could not be achieved without encouraging democracy. Later issues also included an investigation and criticism of the state security system, and an attack on Deng Xiaoping. Its fundamental principle was the desire to explore Socialist alternatives in China, hence the title. The paper temporarily ceased publication after 29th March when Wei Jingsheng, its leading light and a former Red Guard opposed to Jiang Qing, who had previously been imprisoned for three months at the beginning of 1967, was arrested together with other activists.

This poem plays on the topography of Tiananmen Square, where Mao's Mausoleum is to the south, and the former Forbidden City (the Imperial Palace) to the north. The author's pseudonym means 'Skyscraper'.

SPRING WIND
Lü Sun

Of this endless winter's fairytale I've had my fill,
You woke me – never again shall I be perverse.
'People should be like people', of course they will
Strive for life's rights which cannot be transferred.
Kiss all those you love,
You will sweep the dust from off your soul.
Raise your wings again to fly yet farther on,
People will not be content just to breathe freely before this wall.

from *China's Human Rights* February 1979, p. 10

Notes

'China's Human Rights' was the publication of the Human Rights Alliance, formed at the turn of the year. On or around 1st March 1979, the Human Rights Alliance split in two as a result of clashes over both personalities and policies. Some members wanted to concentrate on organizing peasants and petitions at the mass level, others preferred to emphasize publicity through wall-posters and gaining group status and recognition in the National People's Congress. Again, some members were in favour of China's war with Vietnam, others opposed it. After the split both factions continued to produce their own version of 'China's Human Rights' until shortly after the arrests of their leaders between 29th March and 4th April 1979.

Although this poem sounds as though it was written after the end of March 1979 when the activities of the Democracy Movement were limited to the area around Democracy Wall, in fact it is taken from the first issue of 'China's Human Rights', which pre-dated the split.

BEFORE SPRING

We are bound in the fetters of feudalism,
The vapours of superstition fill the air in China,
How can we boast of freedom of speech?
The government's will is a well known dictum.
We are in no way shabbily dressed,
Behind the bars are even peaceful flowerbeds,
But these are the bonds of peace,
We want to create the Spring of Democracy.
The murderers of April 5th stand outside the law,
Modernization walks with difficulty,
The nation's thoughts cannot reach emancipation,
Advancement is only the swindling of man's speech.
Is it progress for all to speak with one voice?
How can one still use a thought to confine the young.
China's been through numbers of disasters,
Today's people want to speak for themselves.
Quickly smash the spiritual shackle of people's minds, that
    Golden Hoop,
Everything withstands the test of practice.
Our urgent campaigns,
Shouted awake the people who, intoxicated with sweetness, are
    easily satisfied,
For China's democracy,
Don't spare the blood of the lives of your own young,
Irrigate the tender shoots of the Chinese nation.
For China's democracy, don't fear the return of miscarriages
    of justice.
Because if there is no Spring of People's Democracy,
The Four Modernizations will be idle talk,
Young people have to get organized
Break through the shackles
Liberate thought
Use actions to draft the Declaration of Democracy.
The April 5th Movement is still but a bud,
Welcome the full bloom of spring,
Wait for the coming year.

from *Science, Democracy and Law* No. 1, p. 11.

Notes

At least partially because the Democracy Movement started during the winter, the coming of spring became an oft repeated symbol for the expansion of democracy. As with much of the Democracy Movement, such calls for greater democracy were not seen by their proponents as resisting the national leadership, but on the contrary as a necessary part of aiding and developing the national goals of the 'Four Modernizations'. They were encouraged in this belief by Deng's implicit approval passed on to a mass meeting in Tiananmen Square at the end of November 1978 through a Canadian journalist, John Fraser of the Toronto Globe and Mail.

IN PRAISE OF THE NEW SPRING

In Beijing, smoke from firecrackers shakes the sky,
And the Spring wind rises from the Democracy Wall.
In the old days, at the Spring Festival, people called on friends
    and relatives,
As today brave men visit the Democracy Wall.
Only heroes chase away fierce beasts,
And frighten to death lackeys and miserable worms.
Debate the truth at the Democracy Wall,
And the new Spring Festival will add lustre to the rainbow.

from *Science, Democracy and Law* No. 5, p. 2.

FROZEN LAND
Meng Ke

The funeral crowd floats past, a white cloud,
Rivers slowly drag the sun.
The long, long surface of the water, dyed golden.
How silent
How vast
How pitiful
That stretch of withered flowers.

from *Today* No. 1, p. 26.

SMOKE FROM THE WHITE HOUSE
Meng Ke

The smoke from the white house
Is fine and long
The woman walks slowly towards the river bank ...

There drifts by a broken mast,
Its surface shattered by a blast.

from *Today* No. 1, p. 27.

References

[1] 'Explanation on Seven Laws', by Peng Zhen, Director of Commission for Legal Affairs of National People's Congress Standing Committee, at Second Session of Fifth National People's Congress on 26 June 1979, in *Beijing Review* No. 28, 13 July 1979, p. 8ff.
[2] *Index on Censorship* Vol. 8, No. 5, p. 3, 'Manifesto of the Alliance for Human Rights in China'.
[3] 'Exploration' No. 2, 29 January 1979, p. 16.
[4] Wall-poster on Democracy Wall, dated 15th March 1979, 'Record of an investigation into the Fu Yuehua Incident by a delegation of Beijing's Mass organizations and publications', signed by 'Masses Reference News', 'April 5th Forum', 'Exploration', Enlightenment Society (Beijing Branch), and the China Human Rights Alliance.

CHAPTER FIVE

March–April 1979: Literary Expression and Political Repression

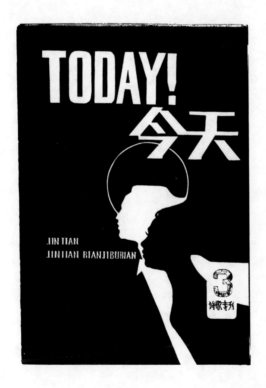

Cover of 'Today' Special Poetry Edition

At the beginning of March 1979 the Democracy Movement appeared buoyant as it prepared for the first official celebration of the Tiananmen Incident on April 5th. A printed, although still unofficial version of 'The Spring of Peking' appeared on 5th March, and most of the unofficial publications were preparing special editions. 'Today', in particular, which had in its first two issues encouraged literary experimentation, was preparing a special poetry only edition for the occasion, and had even made arrangements for it, like 'The Spring of Peking' to be properly printed rather than just mimeographed. In the event, by April 5th all that remained for the Democracy Movement was the choice of literary expression, both political and cultural democracy having been very firmly ruled out of order for the conceivable future.

March started badly with splits occurring in both the Enlightenment Society and the Human Rights Alliance. The Enlightenment Society had originally started in Guiyang with twelve members, four of whom stayed behind while the rest went off to establish branches elsewhere. They arrived in Beijing in November, with mimeographed copies of their original (Guiyang) wall-posters 'Li Yizhe-style'. However, there were clear political and personal difficulties within the group. Having barely managed to establish an independent Beijing branch of the Enlightenment Society, its Guiyang in Beijing branch (the original eight who had come in November)[1] split into three over questions of reform versus revolution and politics versus art and literature. Two new Enlightenment Societies in Beijing were founded, one in favour of political reform, the other for the primacy of a revolution in the arts as the immediate task. The third breakaway group was very opposed to Mao, preferred the road of political revolution and re-named itself 'Thaw' (*Jiedong*). The split in the Human Rights Alliance was somewhat simpler, though it was undoubtedly helped by the presence of an agent provocateur (provided by the public security services) in the Alliance's original three-man leadership group. The two remaining leaders, Chen Lu and Ren Wanding represented different tendencies within the organization and soon split. Ren and his followers argued that the immediate political tasks were to keep writing wall-posters and agitate for gaining group status and recognition in the National People's Congress. At the same time they approved of China's invasion of Vietnam. On the other hand the group led by Chen Lu were against China's war in Vietnam and thought the immediate political tasks should be to continue organizing and aiding 'petitioners' coming to the capital to demonstrate. In both cases, the divisions were not in themselves fatal, but the struggles for control of the original parent bodies' resources diverted their energies at a crucial moment in the Democracy Movement's development.

However, the axe really started to fall on the 15th and 16th March in two speeches given by Deng Xiaoping and Hu Yaobang (the CCP's new Secretary-General) to relatively high-ranking cadres in Beijing. Deng spoke mainly about the war in Vietnam, but he is reported to have said that Fu Yuehua (the Human Rights activist arrested on 18th January) was a 'bad girl and a reactionary' and that she would be given a public trial[2]; and to have defended Mao, reportedly saying 'we must keep Mao, and he shouldn't be overthrown'. This last remark was presumably a defence against the attacks on Mao being made in the official political system, as for example, Lu Dingyi's comments that it was not Peng Dehuai who had been mistaken in 1959 (when he had criticized and attacked Mao personally in an 'open letter' for the latter's handling of the Great Leap Forward) but Peng's critic(s) – that is Mao Zedong[3]. Hu Yaobang for his part was more directly critical of the Democracy Movement, reportedly calling it and Democracy Wall 'rubbish and reactionary' and comparing the activists unfavourably with the young heroes who had been killed at the front during the Sino-Vietnamese War.

Following these speeches, Democracy Movement activists became subject to more intense surveillance by the public security forces. On Monday 19th and Tuesday 20th March, leading officials at the workplaces of Democracy Movement activists (although not the activists themselves) were questioned about the activists' work and social lives. But still there were no arrests. On the other hand, the local *Beijing Daily* (*Beijing ribao*) started to publish a series of articles on human rights and democracy, whose conclusion was obvious. On 22nd March it carried '"Human Rights" is not a proletarian slogan', which stated:

> There is a world of difference between calling for human rights in a socialist as opposed to a feudal society. Originally it was a slogan for the bourgeoisie at the end of the *ancien régime*. The slogan of human rights appears to transcend class but in fact its class nature is clearly capitalist. There are rights and privileges for capitalists only. Our state is the people's own state. We support the people's rights but not those of counter revolutionaries. Those who say 'human rights' have no class nature ... whether subconsciously or deliberately have arrived on the side of the capitalist class. It is incorrect to raise a slogan of wanting human rights under socialism. There is clearly the need to overturn the bad works of the Gang of Four and Lin Piao, but we must be discriminating. Some cases need the verdicts reversing, but this is not so generally – China must stay red and socialist. The call for human rights is linked to calls for a return to capitalism and imperialism. When did these ever serve China well?

This was followed by various articles on similar themes until 29th March when it led with, 'When there are rights there are also obligations'. The central theme of this article was that the individual's rights are made clear in the Constitution: that one must have centralism as well as democracy, discipline as well as freedom, that rights and obligations cannot be separated, and that the people's state implies both rights and obligations. 'But' it went on 'we must recognize that there are a few people, especially a few young people, lacking in social experience.'

It was a warning for some of the Democracy Movement's activists, but for others it was too late. The Beijing

Revolutionary Committee had already adopted regulations for 'democratic' activities, although these were not published for two days[4], and on the same day at least two Democracy Movement activists had been arrested. One was Chen Lu, the other Wei Jingsheng of 'Exploration'. The regulations restricted all activities to the area around Democracy Wall and included an injunction not to attack 'Socialism, the Dictatorship of the Proletariat, leaders of the Communist Party, or Marxism-Leninism-Mao Zedong Thought'. Only four days before, in reaction to Deng Xiaoping's mid-March speech, 'Exploration' had bitterly attacked Deng for the latter's attack on the Democracy Movement:

> Is Deng Xiaoping worthy of the people's trust? ...
> Does Deng Xiaoping want democracy? ... No, he does not ...
> The people must maintain vigilance lest Deng
> Xiaoping becomes a dictator.[5]

Reactions at Democracy Wall the following Sunday (April 1st) ranged from panic and hysteria to annoyance and the desire to expressively retaliate, particularly as plans had been made for the next Thursday – April 5th. But perhaps the most impressive response of all was that of a young man who strode through the crowd, posted his poem on the wall, and then left without saying a word. That poem is 'For You ...', the last presented in this section. For him at least, spring's chill wind had blown.

Events during the following week were very muted, understandably, when compared to late November. Ren Wanding (of the Human Rights Alliance) was arrested in public at Democracy Wall on April 4th, when trying to put up a wall-poster equating human rights with Marxism. The remaining members of 'Exploration' were either arrested or kept well-hidden, and in general most prominent activists kept a low profile. 'Today' managed to produce their special Tiananmen Incident anniversary poetry edition, although in the end it was typewritten onto stencils rather than printed, because Beijing's printing workshops had been warned off handling unofficial publications for the future. April 5th itself passed off quietly enough, with large crowds throughout the day both at Democracy Wall and in Tiananmen Square. There were a few summary and short-lived arrests for minor infringements of the new regulations, but that was all. Finally on Sunday 8th April, there was an open air poetry reading in 'August 1st' Park organized by the 'Today' group in commemoration of the Tiananmen Incident, which passed off totally without incident. But by then almost anything would have been an anti-climax.

CHANG AN STREET
Qi Yun

You told the birch: 'I don't love you anymore.'
Your face against the silver branch: 'Go quick!'
You said: 'Good Luck!'
But you no longer saw my name.
You went from tree to tree
As if you had to count them all.
I still turned my head,
Wanting you to know,
I was crying.

It wasn't long ago,
I still remember those promises,
Only now I don't feel ashamed,
I can't help but ache and cry,
As on the coldest day,
I'm attracted by fire.
Maybe this was only waiting,
But it's worse than waiting,
And maybe that's the hurt.
You don't have to believe me, when I say
I miss you;
Comfort me now –
As always I'm alone.
I know I'll never really forget
You've already become my childhood.

from *Today* No. 3, p. 13.

Notes

'Today' is probably the most professional of all the unofficial publications to have appeared in terms of content, production and organization. Certainly it is the most popular of the literary unofficial magazines. It was started by Meng Ke and Bei Dao (pseudonyms like all the names used by authors in 'Today') as a contribution to greater democracy in literature following the years of the Cultural Revolution. As a result attempts at the experimental are presented alongside more traditional forms. Poetry has formed a substantial part of each issue, and issue number three, published on the anniversary of April 5th, from which this and the following six poems are taken, was a special all-poetry edition. Two of the poets regularly published in 'Today', Bei Dao and Shu Ting, have had poems which were originally published there reprinted in the official magazine *Poetry Monthly*. Bei Dao's 'Reply' appeared in *Poetry Monthly* No. 3 (March 1979), p. 46, and Shu Ting's 'To the Rubber Tree' appeared in *Poetry Monthly* No. 4 (April 1979), p. 56. Both originally appeared in 'Today' No. 1. Because they have appeared in the official press these poems have not been translated here.

AN UNTITLED POEM
Qi Yun

Amidst the rain
Two little birds meet beneath stone ruins.
Carding each other's feathers
preparing to fly high
into the gloomy sky.
Using their beaks
They explore each other,
not wanting to start out
not wanting to finish.

We do not test, we do not praise,
We do not hope, we do not seek.
Evading the wind and rain,
evading love,
wishing to evade everything – if possible.

We can't devote our minds
to so many hopes.
The water can freeze into ice
but it easily melts;
and what's more we all know,
those harbours without a smile
those long journeys with no spring water.
Even if the small boat
possessed more paddles,
the ocean is endless.

Let's embrace
like that pair of little birds
with drenched feathers.
Who wants to fly?
I wish you could fly even higher.

I only wish to see one thing
when we depart
can we have tears on our chapped faces?

from *Today* No. 3, p. 14.

A STORY OF FISH
in three parts.
Shi Zhi

1

Beneath a sheet of frozen ice, fish drift with the flow,
One cannot hear their painful sighs,
Beyond reach of the sun's warm rays,
How can life receive the splendour of sunset or sunrise?!

In reality there are no waves,
So how to carry on the bloody fight?
What can the future hold in store,
The prospect is simply out of sight.

The fish's spirits, there is but one thing to console,
Just to wallow as sweet recollections unfold.
Let the tears of sadness and of joy,
Draw up again from the dim past memories now old.

Yet not to pursue the calyx on the spring tide,
Not beneath the blazing sun to rest serene;
No not the chilly wind of early spring,
Nor midsummer's water rippled green.

But rather to be nature's bloody wound,
Freshly healed and wrapped in white gauze.
On the ground no more restless leaves whirl to and fro,
No more lingering in the sky are traces of frozen snow.

Oh how the fish leap in a furious frenzy
So not to lose the breath of liberty;
Oh how they carry out their fierce resistance,
So not to lose a chance to be free.

Though each time they resist ends in defeat,
Though each time they leap they run into a wall.
Yet the brave fish never lose heart,
And they save their strength to finally give their all.

At last they find a weak link in the chain,
Good, wind up and leap to liberty,
Arched bodies flying in midair,
What strength and what agility.

The water's penetrated by an insipid ray of sun,
Which lightly strokes the fishes' bleeding fins:
'Kids, this is the last we'll see of this year,
I'm afraid the next time we'll meet won't be until next spring!'

The fish merrily leap to meet the sun's warm rays,
At once their heads poke through the ice to catch a breath of
   freedom.
Their fresh blood weaves a red patch in the lazy current,
Their dance soon unfurls a red flag on the battleground
   beneath them.

But suddenly a flash of violent pain,
Knocks the fish senseless, and they sink into the depths below.
My little fish, you are still so young,
How can you end your lives just so.

Don't sink fish, don't sink again,
From the depth of my heart I pray.
... At last the fish are coming to,
And swim madly towards the sun's warm rays.

Sparing nothing, their heads break through the surface,
Their frozen lips still move without a sound.
Until the undulating gurgles are transformed,
Into a lofty voice which thereupon resounds.

'Never fear the cold-hearted wind and snow,
On no account bend to their freezing breath.'
And on that, they plunge down to the bottom,
Without even looking back, swim into the depth ...

Beneath a sheet of frozen ice, fish drift with the flow,
One cannot hear their painful sighs,
Beyond reach of the sun's warm rays,
How can life receive the splendour of sunset or sunrise!

2

By moonlight, the fisherman bores a hole in the ice,
And hastily lays his nets while on the bank,
He piles stores of food and tobacco,
To wait out the green dawn in the mist so dank.

Why do the stars hang like glistening tears?
In this darkness can there be any sentiment?
But why not wait until the fish have had some warning,
Dawn's fingers pluck the scattered icy stars which fill the
    firmament.

A ray of blinding brilliant sunshine,
Dazzles the fish's tightly shut eyes,
And warms the frozen dreams beneath the ice,
Affectionately calling the deep sleeping fish to rise:

'My children, do you still recognize me?
Can you still call my name out right?
Do you still seek your destiny?
Do you still pursue freedom and light?'

The fish, on hearing the sunshine's questions,
Open their eyes so perplexed and depressed,
They try to move their numb little tails,
Their fins now and then beat their breasts:

'Ray of liberty, tell us truly,
Can the spring that we hope for be near?
Can the bait, so hard to swallow, have been placed on the
     bank?
Have the swallows begun to reappear?'

Silence, silence, fearful silence,
They receive not the slightest reply.
The hearts of the fish suddenly tremble,
As they hear the tree branches' whisking cry.

Vigilant, they press at once to the fore,
But still infatuated by the ray of light,
They seek the brilliance of the sun to see clearly,
What the dim future holds in sight.

But the fish lose all hope as they clearly see,
Beside them, the hideous nets are lain.
'Where is spring', they cry, eyes filled with tears,
And they begin their journey beneath the ice again.

Like the fisherman chomping on his food,
The sunlight tears through the greedy nets.
In the mists to which his pipe smoke ascends,
The fisherman dreams of a bountiful harvest.

3

The reviving spring finally comes around,
The sun's sharp sword reveals its power.
Mercilessly carving up the ice-locked river,
On the river bed ice floes crash and flounder.

A python hibernating beneath the ice,
On peeping out, immediately shrinks back to the deep;
The frog, foremost acclaimed singer,
Is frightened and quickly makes a helter skelter leap.

My fish, my little fishies,
Where are you, where can you be?
You've cherished hope through the winter but if you'd died,
Your corpses should float up to me!

Oh fish have you really died,
Eyes like the moon, detached and chill,
Just now a slight quiver of the cheek,
But now, like the waves beneath the surface, still.

Because they are still young, their nature so persistent,
Ardently thirsting after freedom and the sun,
They leap from the water with abandon,
Only to land on a floe which will finally melt and be gone.

Nearly dead the fish struggle madly on the floe,
Behind the clouds the sun hastily withdraws her rays –
With anguish she watches all her little children,
Young fish, so this is how you'll end your days.

The fish give everything to their last request:
'Sun, we are your little fry,
Quickly draw your sharp sword,
With the blocks of ice we're ready to melt and die!'

Dead, the fish are now really dead,
Their eyes are like the cold moon's glow,
A cheek just made a slight quiver,
But now is still like the water's flow.

Green spring leaves one by one,
Though there is no wind, drift down to the ground,
A fine drizzle just like tear drops,
Buries fish corpses without a sound.

A pile of fish bones reveals their glory,
A bounteous spiritual treasury,
On seeing that verdant grave, my spirit,
Cannot but drift into contemplative reverie ...

E

The blocks of ice have melted away,
The river's current no longer boils.
The frog leaps from a clump of grass,
And from her bath the python uncoils.

Her belly full, the python peacefully listens,
To the frog's sympathetic croon.
The python's moved to tears by the tale,
Of how the fish met their doom.

from *Today* No. 3, p. 16.

Notes

This thinly disguised political allegory focuses on an oft-repeated symbol in the Democracy Movement, the coming of spring, but perhaps in a rather different if more cynical vein to the usual. The author's pseudonym means 'Forefinger'.

APRIL DUSK
Shu Ting

In the April dusk
Are strung out the notes of a green melody,
Whirling in the gorges,
Wavering in the sky.
If echoes spill from the soul,
No need to suffer, searching elsewhere.
If you have a song, then sing, but please,
Gently, gently, softly ...

April dusk,
Like a memory lost and recovered,
Perhaps there'll be a meeting
Not scheduled up till now;
Perhaps a time of passionate love
Can never be allowed.
If you have tears, then weep, let the tears
Flow, flow, silently ...

from *Today* No. 3, p. 36.

NOTES FROM THE CITY OF THE SUN
Bei Dao

Life
The sun still rises.

Love
Stillness. Wild geese fly over
virgin waste land.
Old trees topple with a crack.
Sharp, salty rain sprays the air.

Freedom
Float.
Torn scraps of paper.

Child
A balloon lifts its cradle
And flies up and up into the blue.

Girl
A shimmering rainbow
collects birds' coloured feathers.

Youth
Red waves
drench solitary oars.

Art
Millions of shining suns
are reflected in a broken mirror.

The People
The moon has been torn into many glistening ears of grain
sown into honest sky and earth.

Labour
Hands. Enfold the globe.

Fate
Children at random hit railings.
Railings at random hit the night.

Faith
A flock of sheep spill beyond the limits of their pasture,
the shepherd still plays his same old tune.

Peace
In the shop window of a food store
a silent chocolate cannon revolves.

The Motherland
She was engraved on a bronze shield
which leant against a partition in a museum.

Living
A net.

from *Today* No. 3, p. 38.

SONG FROM THE LITTLE WOODEN HOUSE
Bei Dao

for Shanshan on her twentieth birthday

Because of you
Spring is in song.
Grass turns green, flowers red
and small honey bees paddle in their fragrant juices.

Because of you
White poplars bend down to the ground.
Squirrels scamper, cuckoos call
and wake the old grey wolf deep in the thickest forest.

Because of you
Black clouds shake the Milky Way
Rain drops fall, spray flies
and sprinkles intoxicated little rivers.

Because of you
Sailboat clouds fly away driven by the wind.
The tide rushes forward, the waves break
and lap against the little wooden house by the river.

Because of you
The little wooden house opens a window.
Your long-dormant brother wakes at last
and opens his eyes, looks out of the window.

Because of you
A light filters in through the small window.
He dips his pen in the red ink of his heart
and writes down this poorly-written poem.

from *Today* No. 3, p. 40.

Notes

Shanshan was Bei Dao's younger sister.
She died in her twenty-third year when trying to rescue a friend who
was drowning in Beiyang, a lake in northern Hebei province.

LET'S GO
Bei Dao

for L.

Let's go,
Fallen leaves have flown into deep valleys
But the sounds of song have no home to go to.

Let's go,
Moonlight on ice
Overflows the riverbed.

Let's go,
Eyes towards the one patch of sky
The heart beats the drum of dusk.

Let's go,
We didn't forget
We will find the lake of life.

Let's go,
Road, oh road
Swaying with red opium poppies.

from *Today* No. 3, p. 42.

THE GREAT SEA

After producing one more
Heaven shattering earth shaking roar,
it now again
returns to calm.

The low sweeping pitchblack curtain of night
uses its strong sturdy chest
to push down the head of the great sea
trying to suffocate its freedom to breathe;
and the great sea is actually so silent
that it seems to have already submitted to darkness.

Lying half submerged the jagged vicious rocks
like pile on pile of jet black monsters
in frenzied ferocious motion on the surface of the sea
reveal their sharp teeth
and stretch out their innumerable pairs of iron claws;
and the great sea actually seems to have shut its eyes
bowing its head to their despotic power.

After the great sea had been in the dark some time
in the immeasurable gloom
it seemed as if it would actually
pass out altogether ...

Quiet and dark are ruling the world
formless flowing elements
which seem to solidify to form
a tangible whole
and the great sea –
are you in deep sleep – or
are you storing up your invincible power,
awaiting the return of the hurricane?

As the heavens take off
their dark overcoat
on the distant eastern backdrop of sky
flashes a majestic star, a strange ray of light;
this is the dawn nymph – the daughter of Aurora

who uses a soft voice to tell the great sea
'Time to get up!'
The great sea hearing this friendly call
actually starts to come round
it opens its bright eyes
and slowly raises its head.

Now the beautiful first light of day
kisses the great sea's forehead
Then hurriedly flies off
to beyond the coastline.
A sudden breeze springs up
to meet with the great sea's embrace,
then hurriedly takes its leave
to go to join the birds and the clouds.

The light of the morning clouds stirs its spirit.
The wind brashly jolts its corporal frame.
It is completely awake now – and
it again starts its deep roar of rage.

A great wind suddenly blew
along came thunder and lightning,
and the great sea angrily flexes its body
that magnificent laugh makes the dark clouds and the rocks
    tremble in fright.
'You tried to crush my element of freedom, did you?'
'You tried to use frightening faces to threaten me, did you?'
Questioning the steely grey sky and the jet black rocks
his voice shakes the entire universe
and the sky and rocks tremble with fear.

The great sea rages and roars,
'Didn't you try to strangle me
you forced me to submit to the dark
but now you are trembling aren't you?
Huh! Don't lose heart, come and pit your strength against
me!'

He then raises a gigantic heaven flooding breaker
and in a flash

a crashing deluge like a great army speeds up to the sky
and that flood of light
destroys the darkness and swallows the rocks.
It is like a mass of torches
lighting up bright the whole of the earth.

The dark sky
amid the enraged roar of the great sea
is pitifully shattered.
The ugly rocks
amid the fiercesome deluge of the waves
leave only a fear of ignominious defeat, a cry for mercy.

The great sea raises its head aloft and puffs out its chest,
It is going to roar out in anger once again!
After a night of darkness – then
it will wash away all tyrannical intimidation
to take all the evil force which constrains it
for burial in that grave which lies under its feet.

(5th April 1979) from *Live* No. 1, p. 41.

DON'T THINK I'M TRYING TO GET AT YOU

Weeds do not make garlands,
Ants do not make coursers,
And nobody can lift a ton;
Don't overestimate your own resources.
My brother, oh my brother,
You should be sincere,
Big talk is not so nice to hear.

You drive a donkey and that is clear,
Yet you say you've been round the hemisphere.
When you only rise at mid-morn,
You still say you got up with the crack of dawn.
My brother, oh my brother,
There's no need to fantasize,
Don't tell us any lies.

I mention this and you'll pull a long face,
You say you are goodness pure and true,
You don't love me but take it in bad grace,
But don't think I'm trying to get at you.
My brother, oh my brother,
You should talk honestly,
Relatives are after all a family.

I want you to get up earlier and retire later,
I want your mind broader and your ambitions greater.
It's not nice to hear but I mean well for you,
I only hope you'll hear me through.
My brother, oh my brother,
I do truly love you,
With all my heart I love you.

from *Dandelion* No. 4, p. 1.

MY HUSBAND'S MOTHER

I go up the hill to take the sheep to roam,
But you drag me back to stay round the home.
When I go to the fields to cut the grass,
You turn right around and call me an ass.

Don't stand at my door,
Don't lay down the law.
Dear head of the household,
Dear mother-in-law.

I have always found hard work appeals,
But you call me back to cool my heels.
When I've a few questions I want to pose,
You turn right around and stamp on my toes.

Don't stand at my door,
Don't lay down the law,
Dear head of the household,
Dear mother-in-law.

from *Dandelion* No. 4, p. 1

'FOR YOU ...'
Ling Bing

My friend,
Parting time is pending.
Farewell – Democracy Wall.
What can I briefly say to you?
Should I speak of spring's frigidity?
Should I say that you are like the withered wintersweet?

No, I ought instead to talk of happiness,
Tomorrow's happiness,
Of pure orchid skies,
Of golden wild flowers,
Of a child's bright eyes.
In sum we ought
To part with dignity,
Don't you agree?

Winter, November.
The bitter cold drives me to your presence.
You use your ash-grey wall to embrace me,
and your ash-grey eyes to say to me,
'Purity, Fraternal Love, Hope'.
You quietly tell me,
'Why not start a bonfire
So that children need never feel the cold again.'
My heart dissolves.
On the wall
A small red fire can't help but rise.

There is an old man.
Passing by, he says to me,
'Child, don't be giddy.
It's a fleeting fancy,
A reflection of yourself.'
My heart, weeping goes straight to you,
'No, it's not a fancy.
It's not a water's upside-down reflection.
It's you,
You – Democracy Wall.'

Perhaps a few more days
And I will sit
Beneath a window, surrounded by iron bars.
Then there will be stares rigid as ice.
Those who come and go will cross-examine me.
They won't understand why
You and I can be as one.

I will cry out with a loud voice to them,
No, to the world, and say,
'You ... in fact ... are ... me,'
The gentle dreams of my childhood,
Little Red Riding Hood, Cinderella and Snow White,
A warrior's avenging sword,
People's best intentions,
A heart dripping with blood.

Perhaps one day
I will be forced to part with you.
At that time,
I will make sport with the stars,
The sky will be my canvas,
The landscape, my stringed instrument.
I will sing with a loud voice
Of beautiful harmonic rhyme, of the ravings of love,
Of you, of glorious nature, of hope.

I believe
That you will not vanish,
That you will not die.
In the frightened eyes of children,
Where grown men droop their heads,
In every living human heart,
In all these places I have seen you
– You, towering like a mountain peak,
You, thundering as the oceans roar.
Remember,
So long as there is humanity, then surely there is You.

(1st April 1979) from *The Spring of Peking* No. 5, p. 30.

Notes

The author's pseudonym means 'Icicle'. The imagery of Little Red Riding Hood, Cinderella, and Snow White, are not, as one might reasonably assume, the product of free translation, but rather further evidence suggestive of the social background of the Democracy Movement's activists.

References

[1] See the Front covers of 'Enlightenment' (Guiyang Branch) Nos. 1 and 2, where all eight names are listed.
[2] As indeed she has. See SWB FE 6249/BII/11 19 October 1979, NCNA (in English) 17 October 1979.
[3] RMRB 8 March 1979, p. 2.
[4] *Beijing ribao* (*Peking Daily*) 31 March 1979, p. 1. 'Notice of Beijing Municipality Revolutionary Committee, 29 March 1979'.
[5] 'Do we want Democracy or Dictatorship?' by 'Exploration' Editorial Board. Wall-poster on Democracy Wall, 24 March 1979, and 'Exploration', Special Edition, 25 March 1979.

CHAPTER SIX

The Democracy Movement, November 1978 – April 1979: An Assessment

'The Spring of Peking' on sale, April 5th 1979

The very existence of this book would seem to suggest that the Democracy Movement was an event of some considerable importance. However, it is easy to both overestimate and underestimate the Democracy Movement's significance. It would be easy to overestimate, because in many ways the Democracy Movement was essentially a marginal and limited phenomenon in purpose, effect and participation. On a rough estimate the total number of hardcore activists in Beijing (excluding those who only contributed articles etc. to unofficial publications) cannot have exceeded many more than two hundred. Moreover, it has been suggested that most were drawn from a very narrow and cohesive social category; namely those whose pre-Cultural Revolution socialization had given them expectations which were hardly likely to be fulfilled during 1966-76. Throughout Beijing the Democracy Movement attracted wide interest. However, interest is not the same as support. The support that was generated was more generally for the concept of greater freedom rather than necessarily for the specific activities of the Democracy Movement.

Indeed reactions to Democracy Movement activities by the general citizenry of Beijing were not so very different to those experienced by youthful demonstrators in the West. On the whole there was a marked lack of support from other social categories. Strangely enough, even that social category who might have been assumed to have most to gain from the Democracy Movement and therefore to be most involved and in its vanguard – namely, the recently re-instated intellectuals (whether they had been in disgrace since 1957 or the GPCR) have not only studiously avoided involvement, they have been disparaging to a large extent. The explanation for this paradox is not hard to find – they are concerned lest the waves from the Democracy Movement rock the boat of their new found intellectual freedom.

The lack of involvement by other social groups, and particularly the intellectuals, and other aspects of the Democracy Movement's marginality and limitations are explicitly recognized and admitted by a leader of one of the Democracy Movement's leading organizations in an essay entitled 'What are the implications of China's Democratic Experiment?' Written and released shortly before his arrest, it is presented at the end of this section, not because it is *the* authentic voice of the activist but merely because it is one voice among others that may never be heard. Remarkable for both its style and political sophistication, this piece concludes that the Democracy Movement failed because it neither attempted, nor was allowed to escape the marginality which, because of the nature of the state and the state's hold over society during the previous thirty years, was its necessary genesis. Yet there is still hope expressed, as with the poem 'Trust the Future' – originally written in the dark literary days of the early 1970s.

Moreover, the Democracy Movement was limited because of its distinct lack of cohesion. The cry was for freedom and democracy but its aims were always unclear. The shape of any possible future democracy was a problem which elicited many different responses on the few occasions when it was addressed. Statements have ranged from attacks on the 'Gang of Four' through requests for redressal of personal grievances and support for Hua, Deng and the CCP, to arguments for capitalism, Christianity and so on. It would thus clearly be wrong to view the Democracy Movement as a broad-based mass movement of revolt against the CCP.

On the other hand, the Democracy Movement should not be dismissed as merely the expressivism of a load of semi-literate workers, degenerates, street ruffians and prostitutes, as the CCP and the Democracy Movement's critics all too frequently suggested. In the first place, the Democracy Movement was part of a much larger social movement which started in the summer of 1978 or perhaps even earlier. This larger social movement has led to the questioning of China's past, present and future to such an extent that not only has it created a real and sustained revolution in officially published literature, but it has also led amazingly to the political reassessment of at least the last twenty years and possibly longer[1]. The activities of the Democracy Movement may have been frowned on, but the drive for greater freedom was not. It was, and to a large extent remains, a debate on tactics rather than strategy.

Secondly, an important part of this requestioning has been the social reforms which have followed in the wake of the fall of the 'Gang of Four'. As has already been suggested, to all intents and purposes there has been a Counter Cultural Revolution. Those who were removed from power and influence or punished during the GPCR have been reinstated and recompensed. But the *status quo ante* has not been completely restored. There remains at least one highly underprivileged social group, namely those young people, who are now in their late twenties and thirties, and who because of the educational policies of the GPCR, never had the chance to complete their education. Instead they were 'sent down to the front line of production', mainly in the countryside to 'learn from the peasants'[2]. At first it was implied that such a policy would only result in temporary displacements. However, as the years passed very few of the 'rusticated' youth managed to return either to their studies or their home cities. During 1978/9 their discontent became an explosive issue, particularly in Shanghai. Returning home for the Spring Festival (Chinese New Year) celebrations, many staged demonstrations, including a sit-in at the railway station, and refused to return to the countryside.[3] Although not 'sent down to the countryside' the Democracy Movement's activists are an important part of that generation displaced by the GPCR. For the most part they were able to avoid complete 'rustication' through their own or family connections. However, as a corollary their relative deprivation was in fact greater than those who were 'sent down to the countryside'. As children of relatively well-placed cadres and intellectuals before the GPCR they had higher educational and life-style expectations. Not only have their grievances from the GPCR not been redressed, but as the 'underprivileged privileged' they are in fact the most articulate and organized of their generation. For this reason and this reason alone the Democracy Movement has to be taken seriously. Its activists are the tip of an iceberg. Here is the real 'lost generation' of the Cultural Revolution – as opposed to those leading cadres removed from office during the GPCR but more recently rehabilitated – demanding their share of the 'new' *status quo*, and almost whatever happens to the Democracy Movement, the problem of that 'lost generation' will remain for the conceivable future.

TRUST THE FUTURE
Shi Zhi

When spiders' webs mercilessly sealed up my stove,
When the ashes of my last cigarette sighed with the sorrow of
    poverty,
I stubbornly still sowed the ashes of lost hope,
With beautiful snowflakes I wrote: Trust the future.

When purple grapes became deep autumn's dew,
When my bouquet was held in someone else's arms,
I stubbornly still took the wet withered vine
On desolate earth to write: Trust the future.

I want to point with my finger to the lines of waves rushing
    towards the horizon,
With the palm of my hand to raise up the ocean of the sun,
Flickering light of dawn, that beautiful warm writing brush,
With childlike strokes I write: Trust the future.

The eyes of the people who trust in the future
Make me firmly believe in the future myself –
Their eyelashes bat off the dust of history,
Their pupils pierce the years of writings.

No matter what people think about our rotting flesh,
That sadness of a lost way, that pain of defeat,
I don't care if they're moved to tears in deep sympathy
Or whether they sneer and laugh with contempt.

I strongly trust people fairly to assess
Our countless explorations, errors, successes, failures,
To judge our will in a warm-hearted, objective way.
Yes, I anxiously await their judgement.

Friend, trust firmly in the future,
Trust in unyielding effort,
Trust in the victory of youth over death,
Trust the future, trust life.

from *Today* No. 2, p. 6.

Notes

Although published for the first time in 'Today' No. 2, 'Trust the Future' was originally written during the Cultural Revolution, and circulated privately around 1970/1. The author's pseudonym means 'Forefinger'.

WHAT ARE THE IMPLICATIONS OF CHINA'S DEMOCRATIC EXPERIMENT?

(The following essay was written by a leader of one of the Democracy Movement's leading organizations shortly before his arrest in May 1979.)

Our generation of Chinese young people has been continually surrounded and enveloped from birth to maturity by the same brand of clamorous propagandist education. When we look at history and consider the various analogous tyrannies of the spirit and culture, ignoring for now other forms of tyranny, it is quite plain that the so-called communist education which the Chinese Communist Party (CCP) has imposed on the youth of China, backed up by all the methods of modern technology, forcibly suppressing all other peaceful systems of thought, theories and even opinions which contain the slightest doubts about the present government, actually boils down to one point: unification through violence. China's youth has been taught that not only must the activities and movements of people be unified but that so must their souls and innermost thoughts be similarly united. Who are the people who will actually lead and direct this unprecedented 'great unity'? 'That's us', say the leaders of the CCP, pointing at themselves, 'we Communists use

*Marxism-Leninism-Mao Zedong Thought to unify the world and to
unify everything!'*

From the latter part of November, 1978, beginning with the Beijing
Democracy Wall, a rebellion burst forth among a section of China's
youth. A rebellion which went completely against the communist teaching
of 'unified will and unified action': a rebellion which caused a severe
historical shock because of its ideological content.

On March 16, 1979, the man who is in practical terms the CCP's top
decision maker, Deng Xiaoping, furiously condemned the spontaneous
rebel movement of the previous four months and issued a threat to suppress
it with violence. On March 29, the Public Security Bureau of Beijing,
basing itself on the premise provided by the explicit declaration of the
Shanghai Public Security Bureau that it would use force to put down the
movement — the so-called principle of 'resorting to force only after
exhausting all peaceful means' — arrested Wei Jingsheng, an important
figure from 'Exploration', one of Beijing's unofficial publications. This
was the first open arrest, on a charge of counter revolution, of a
participant in the rebel movement of the previous four months. Swiftly
following this came searches of all unofficial publications and
organizations, the confiscation of equipment and the detention,
summonsing and interrogation of members of these groups and the formal
arrest of the leaders. A completely spontaneous, peaceful and democratic
experiment met with completely organized and violent suppression. Once
again, tens of thousands of Chinese saw for themselves the reality of
events such as these.

As a youth who for the first time threw himself into the midst of such a
spontaneous movement full of enthusiasm and naive hope and who now is
forced to try to evade arrest by the police of the CCP government I very
much wish simply and quickly to sum up my thoughts up to the present.

1. The challenge to 'Communism' itself.

*Tyranny and dictatorship will not go unchallenged forever. Over the past
30 years the CCP has more than once encountered resistance from the
peaceful masses to its fanatical idea of unified wills and unified action
(unified, that is, through force). This is also not the first time that the
next generation 'educated and nurtured' by the CCP have resisted the 'old
revolutionaries' who educated and nurtured them. Although, if we look at
many of the unprecedented special features of the present movement it is*

the first occasion of its kind. The creative significance of this spontaneous democratic movement is this: It is the first time that China's 'second generation' has spontaneously offered a challenge to the 'Communism', which has over the past decades been looked up to as a sacred standard. Confronting the widespread corruption, absurdity, stagnation, stupidity and backwardness brought about by CCP rule, those who have been participating in the Democracy Movement can basically be divided ideologically into two groups: The first, who believe that this is the result of the failure of the CCP leadership to follow the principles of true Marxism-Leninism and the second, who believe that the CCP leadership has indeed followed the principles of Marxism-Leninism, the terrible thing being that it is precisely this Marxism-Leninism itself which is absurd and erroneous. The first opinion represents the most commonly used method of resistance to the tyrannical rule of the CCP by many people over the past 30 years; but as to what can be regarded as the miracle-working true 'Marxism-Leninism', there are as many opinions as there are people. Over the past decade the Chinese people, including the CCP government, have frequently resorted to bloody fighting resulting in many deaths or injuries over precisely this question. The CCP is a dictatorial clique which believes in the use of force to subdue people, it has incomparably stronger resources of propaganda, organization and forced education than any other person or spontaneous organization in China. Moreover, it has military force with which to carry out suppression. It has been fooling the masses for years and it has a wealth of experience in telling monstrous lies and using the people.

It's only natural, therefore, that in order to achieve victory in 'debate' it resorts to such old devices of tyranny as 'a lie told a thousand times becomes the truth' and 'quantity overcomes quality' and so on. The ordinary people are helpless against tyrannical government. Moreover, Marxism-Leninism is full of contradictions and internal inconsistencies. Time and time again there have been 'creative developments' which have resulted in two sides emerging, both of which claim to be the real Marxism-Leninism and mutually reviling and abusing one another. We have seen many farces of this kind.

The second opinion is clear and simple: Marxism in itself is no good. Those youths holding this view who participated in the Democratic Movement were in the minority. Their attempts at raising clear and definite doubts and opposition to Marxism-Leninism were certainly not particularly lucid or deep. But they did raise the first battle cry to burst through the ideological and spiritual fetters and bonds. Whoever has lived in China under the dictatorship of the proletariat and who is at the same time willing to examine carefully the thinking and spiritual condition of the people will certainly feel most acutely the turbidity and oppressiveness, the quite suffocating atmosphere. The people have been cut off from the outside world for years, cut off from history and no-one is allowed to think freely. From the cradle to the grave, people are only allowed to believe — indeed must believe — in one 'ism'. All else is criminal except to read the one type of 'philosophy', to laud one type of system, to fawn on one leader and to curry favour with one political party. This is particularly true of the second generation, those who have been born in socialist new China. How naive and innocent they are but at the same time how miserable and poor, stagnant and pathetic. They come into the world innocent and without stain and are completely powerless to resist the propaganda of the Marxist 'great Unity', which constantly corrodes and infiltrates their hearts and minds. There is no way for them to embrace any exciting and colourful fantasies. From their tenderest years, they march in the direction of society because the so-called 'all unifying' Marxism-Leninism education, together with punishments and threats have already become essential to their existence. Youths have been trained in such a fashion that they unconsciously quote the doctrines and holy writ of Marxism-Leninism and naturally roll out the Marxism-Leninism world view to impose it upon human life and the world. They are pathetic: they have never had the right to be free — we are told that Marxism-Leninism is true freedom and yet the youth of China are not permitted to take one step outside the confines of this predestined 'ism'. How can they understand human life and the world we live in with its boundless variety? Even the cut of one's clothes, the tunes of songs, the contents of books, the time and place of one's romantic liaisons are all monopolized by the CCP and made the subject of regulations. Just think how much of one's own spirit is left to someone who has lived in such an environment for decades? Indeed, the scars left by a forcible education in Marxism-Leninism's great unity are evident in every debate, every argument and every attempt to be serious on the part of Chinese youth. These are deep-furrowed spiritual scars, and yet, against all expectations, there are people who have dared to organize and resist. Almost unbelievably, from the end of 1978 to early 1979 a few youths emerged who dared to openly proclaim 'we approve of free debate between all philosophies, we do not reverse any existing philosophy or system, we have no reverence for Marxism. We want to seek out for ourselves the road to a prosperous motherland'. In this China, filled with the clamour about Marxist-Leninist great unity, it is difficult to imagine that anyone could hear this without being astonished. People have accused these youths of being arrogant and presumptuous in the extreme, and they have accused them of trying to please the public with claptrap, but there were also those who did not revile them and who sympathized with them. Regardless of the reaction, this is the first time in many years that such a declaration has been made. The cry tells those lost in slumber and reminds those only pretending to be asleep, that there is more than one road in life! Perhaps faith in Marxism-Leninism, the socialist system, rule of the Communist Party, and the dictatorship of the proletariat is a viable way regardless of how many innocent white bones have been buried beneath it — but why is no second way allowed? Or a third, tenth, hundredth, or an infinity of different paths? We Chinese have already met with disaster and grave difficulties on this road which people call Marxism-Leninism; why then can we not try otherwise? The youths who uttered this childish battle cry began to criticize Marxist theory, socialism and the communist system from the point of view of those whose attitude was scepticism or loathing; they are, after all, people who have hewn out a new direction from the oppression, gloom, hesitation and vacillation of the life of modern Chinese youth. However vague the future which this way points may appear today, it is certainly the first fresh and new attempt. For thirty years, year after year China's youth has endured the bitterness of being enclosed, of doctrinal rigidity, of boredom and ossification. Why have there not been more amongst them to come forward with this sort of new experiment? How could it be imagined that in this nation of 4000 years of culture and tradition, with a population of 1000 million, countless numbers of the younger generation would forever have been lost, forcibly enslaved by the theory of 'great unity'. The reverberations of this effort to burst open the doors of the minds of China's youth in order to seek truth through the call to conduct 'free exploration' will echo through the memory of history for a long time to come. The CCP government repeatedly tries to fool itself and fool the people, making a great clamour to the effect that these youths are 'a small handful of counter revolutionary class enemies with ulterior motives' —

but who does not know that only yesterday these rebellious youths were, every one of them, resolutely proclaiming themselves to be 'believers in Marxism-Leninism'. It was none other than the CCP itself which, through its barbaric punitive campaigns forcibly to impose unity, awoke them. The use of violence to suppress free experiment is not only the depth of moral turpitude but it creates a horrifying emptiness in the style of life. Boredom, dullness, desperation, useless schools, imitation, blind obedience, slavery and confinement. The younger generation are richly endowed with the desire not to be enslaved. Their desire is increased by the repeated failures of the CCP administration. Thus resistance to enforced unity is inevitable. If it does not appear today then it will appear tomorrow.

In fact, although the immature views of those who disbelieve or criticize Marxism-Leninism did not convince the majority of those who participated in the Democratic Movement, yet nearly all those who enthusiastically took part conceded that it was good to have free debate. Throughout history, free debate has been absolutely forbidden by most Marxist authorities. Marx, Engels, and Lenin sternly banished all unorthodox or dissenting opinions from within their own groups. At that time, in a situation where adverse external pressure threatened their own existence this harsh 'unifying' activity could be understood to some extent. However, how should one deal with peaceful debate over ideology and practice in the socialist society of the future when outside threats to its existence have basically been removed? With regard to this question, the three great teachers of Marxism-Leninism left no 'far sighted instructions', whereupon such great creative inheritors as Stalin and Mao came along. As soon as power was in their hands they spared no effort to wipe out all opposition. Looking at all Marxist regimes throughout the world there is not one which does not use violence to suppress peaceful opposition. China's spontaneous Democracy Movement which began at the end of 1978 boldly opposed such barbaric, mediaeval, religious-cum-fascist authority. It certainly posed a direct challenge to communism itself.

2. Audacious Spontaneity

The Democracy Movement of late 1978 drew on the remaining prestige of the Tiananmen Incident of early 1976. Those who took part in the Democracy Movement recognized clearly the deep and lasting influence of the Tiananmen Incident and they frequently took the continuation of the April Fifth Movement as their rallying cry. But in practice the Democracy Movement differed from the April Fifth Movement in many ways. In breadth and extent of the question with which it concerned itself this movement was the first of its kind for thirty years. People for the first time broke the unchanging rule of the CCP that the supreme leader was sacred and inviolable, and the first shots were fired directly at the 'great teacher' Chairman Mao who for several decades had occupied an inviolable and omnipotent position. Once this taboo was broken nothing could be held back or forbidden any longer in this ancient nation which had been forcibly reduced to silence. People brought every social issue under discussion, from whether the director of a workshop should be elected and removed from office at fixed intervals to the superiority or otherwise of socialism; the debate very quickly developed from the first stage of individual complaints, personal attacks and controversies about various individual leaders to concentrate on the vital question of how to reform the social system. The April Fifth Movement had no organization and relied on individual efforts but the Democracy Movement quickly evolved into forms of organization based on unifying participants around the publication of magazines. This then developed a further stage where the various groups engaged in joint activities which demonstrated more clearly than ever people's realization of the futility of working separately. Again, through many phenomena such as the establishment of links with foreign public opinion, the organizations of lecture and discussion meetings, etc., this movement demonstrated the close relationship on the one hand between breadth and depth and, on the other hand, audacious spontaneity. All these special features eloquently express a single truth: the Chinese people strongly resist the tyranny of 'great unity', 'we want democracy, we don't want dictatorship', people cried out excitedly. Although the question 'what sort of society is really democratic' was the subject of ceaseless debate and many people were very confused, almost none amongst those who participated in the movement doubted any longer that Chinese society is now and has been for the past few decades a dictatorship. As the movement advanced, the doubts of various groups in society were progressively overcome. This spontaneous criticism from amongst the masses implied opposition to the total uniformity of the past which muzzled all criticism. Therefore in fact it was a declaration of war against the CCP's unity of will and unity of action and it is precisely this which until now has formed the concrete and explicit content of the 'democracy' young people have been shouting about.

3. The Importance of Theory

No political movement can hope to succeed unless it is guided by a mature theory; and it is this problem of theory that was one of the special features of the Democracy Movement. It is quite apparent that a fanatical passion for one particular developed theory on the part of young people cannot be numbered as one of the reasons for the development of the movement. In fact, it came about almost entirely as the result of everybody's anger over the tragic and backward reality of our motherland. Throughout the period of the movement's development, right up until the time when it was forcibly suppressed by the government, none of the participants were able to come up with a mature theory. True, in contemporary China it is impossible to get away from the all-embracing theoretical system of Marxism-Leninism-Mao Zedong Thought. However, virtually all those who participated in the Democracy Movement denied the validity of the official interpretation of and the glosses on this theory. But in practice, the only theoretical system which has matured to the point where it can be put into practice in contemporary China is just this official version of Marxism-Leninism-Mao Zedong Thought. Those who wished to unearth the true Marxism-Leninism in order to oppose it to the official version, were severely hampered not only by lack of time, of strength and of physical equipment, but also by the poverty of imagination brought about by decades of official Marxism-Leninism education. Those who adopted a posture critical of Marxism-Leninism were not only hampered by similar problems but by an even greater lack of material resources — there were simply no books or materials — and by the influence on their morale of the great fear and terror which they felt. Apart from these factors, even more important was the fact that the number of those who, in the midst of the movement, could clearly recognize the importance of a guiding theory, and who, moreover, were resolved to spare no efforts to put it fearlessly into practice, were from first to last all too few. People either wished to, or did, bury themselves in concrete organizational tasks which had to be done or in work of a routine nature and simply had no spare time. In practice, no theory can be established and grow to maturity in the course of a few short months and it was this which led to the tragic result of this spontaneous movement for democracy: there was no developed system which could serve as an ideological standard, uniting convincing argument with a powerful appeal to the people. Many sympathizers felt themselves to be in the dark, and many, who enthusiastically participated, were vague and confused in their thinking. Granted that the tyranny and dictatorship of the CCP was bad, what sort of 'democratic' society should China establish? From beginning to end there was never and perhaps never could have been a new model of society brought forward with which to appeal to and attract the people. Even amongst the most resolute participants in the movement there were those who believed that there was no necessity to set up a model, that it was enough simply to enumerate one by one specific suggestions for social reform. The result was that although the official theoretical system of the communist party must bear the blame for countless disasters, yet it is still the only system which the masses can grasp as a whole, and it is still the only 'sacred' cause which can be used to incite naive youth to devote themselves to struggle. It has no all-round challenge and resistance directed at its core, and it is at the same time a theory which is supported by all the techniques of modern propaganda. It is obvious that it will always have the upper hand whenever confronted in debate over isolated points, specific provisions or concrete individual demands. Modern China is physically poor and the great majority of its inhabitants, regardless of whether they live in the towns or the countryside, have no leisure in which to enjoy the pleasures of intellectual life. Moreover, formal education has to a startling degree taken on the nature of a stupid and drab political religion. Thus, the majority of the Chinese people cannot within a short period of time spontaneously assent to the call to oppose the official administration. Although dissatisfaction with official incompetence is widespread, nowhere can be seen what sort of new society should replace the existing order. If we wish to arouse the masses, we can only do so by adopting a new system with which to oppose the existing official system, and using it to appeal to the people. Precisely because such a new system had simply not matured, the tragic nature of the Democracy Movement was determined from within itself. It could shock, but it had little hope of success, because nobody knew just what sort of a situation success implied.

Theoretical immaturity also led to organizational weakness. The cry to 'destroy the old' is inadequate as a unifying force because whoever seriously participates in the struggle must try to be constructive at the same time as criticizing and destroying.

It is quite true that specific projects, such as publishing magazines, striving for basic human rights etc., united quite a few people but if the call could have been based on a relatively more all-embracing and integrated theory of both destruction and construction, then it would certainly have been possible to unite and influence more people and we would undoubtedly have been more able to organize youth, with its abundance of enthusiasm, in a better and sounder fashion, in order to resist the tyrannical government's oppression and slaughter.

4. The Illusions of Youth

Very few of those who participated in the movement did not entertain excessive illusions; the illusion which did the gravest damage was that which people entertained in respect of the government's repression. Practically from first to last, everybody was continually reminding one another to be vigilant, but at the same time, almost nobody made any detailed arrangements about how to resist arrest, how to be able to continue to print! This was the case in Beijing: we cannot say the same about other cities e.g. Shanghai. A great many of the participants mistakenly believed that repression would not come immediately. In times of peace, people always cherish the illusion that atrocity and outrage are impossible. Young people participating in the first few struggles always seem to have an unrealistic notion of 'cruelty'. Some people maintained that repression would certainly be prefaced by warning signs, some believed that the force of popular sympathy would be sufficient to hold back those within the government advocating repression, others considered the influence of international opinion, while still others reckoned on internal divisions within the CCP ... The result of this was that, when the crackdown came, it immediately became impossible to continue to resolutely publish and proclaim any sharp criticism of the CCP's rule. Nobody had taken steps to prepare a second, secret set of printing equipment. All those who had engaged in penetrating criticism of the government had revealed themselves openly, and were in consequence from that time on unable to escape: constantly being followed and kept under supervision or the danger of search and arrest at any time. Why had nobody taken sufficient precautions? In the first place, this was due to the failure to fully recognize the cruelty of the CCP's armed repression. Nobody had really understood that today's peaceful struggle was only the first step in a protracted and resolute resistance to tyranny and despotism: so that it was vital during this unique and peaceful initial stage to make preparations for the secret struggle which would follow on the repression. Secondly, it was because some people were over-optimistic about the internal and international situation. They believed that the pressure of sympathy from the average citizen, together with the pressure of opinion, would be sufficient to put off the CCP's violent repression. Thirdly because of the weakness of the forces available to the various organizations, all human and material resources had to be thrown into the immediate work of the day, and it was very difficult to release any effective strength in order to make serious preparations for secret work. As the proverb has it, preparedness averts peril; but our preparations were insufficient and our illusions too many, so that our illusions eventually led us into danger. ·

5. The Movement's Participants

The great majority were young workers who had not been to university, most of whom were aged between 20 and 30. Their educational level was that of lower middle school and above. Why were there so few participants of other types? Because of, one, the caution of people of more mature years; two, the arrogance of the intellectuals who believed that the educational level of the workers was too low; three, the ignorance of the situation on the part of the peasants. There is also another problem. That is, why so few young intellectuals, university students, teachers etc. took part in the Democracy Movement, especially those whose age and experience was virtually identical with the people who did participate. The reason is simple: they had just been graced with favours from the CCP government – preferential treatment for intellectuals. It really is pathetic: the CCP, which has over the past decades inflicted every type of maltreatment and suffering on the intellectuals now alters its countenance, be it ever so little, casually flings a few apparently juicy bones into the air, whereupon hordes of young people, and this includes me, immediately join the scramble for tit-bits. It is nothing but examinations, examinations, examinations, as if one's very life depended on them. The one fear is that one might not get into University, not become a research student, not be promoted to technician. It is not that young people are not sceptical of, or repelled by, the leadership of the

CCP, which has created catastrophe and disaster one after another, but wherever they look they see the immensity of the communist party system, and how difficult it is to shake it to its foundations; and even if it were possible to do so, then what sort of a new society should be sought? They do not know. So, many people are vague and uncertain while many others sincerely believe in the CCP's empty slogan of the 'four modernizations'. When you add to this such attractions as the comfortable circumstances of their individual lives, the notion that 'it is safest to engage in technology and the natural sciences' and so on, the result is that the majority of these young people who have either entered university or are in the process of entering university are unwilling to join the movement.

Conclusion

The cry 'we want democracy not dictatorship' has now subsided through-out the vast land of China. Our ancient and immense motherland is still struggling in a mire of poverty and ignorance. But look! The rulers who created this poverty and ignorance are already panicking. They rely on their 'invincible' dictatorship of blood and iron, and yet a few little sheets of paper and a few lines of writing, a few shouts and they're frightened out of their wits. As if confronting a major catastrophe, they trail people, seize belongings, search and arrest: those with right on their side use reasons to convince people, but how can the communist rulers dare to use reason? At a loss for words, with no valid arguments, and shamed into anger, their resort to such violent and atrocious behaviour simply demonstrates the bankruptcy of their position. For the moment they use their swords to cut the throats of others; but remember, this is not the first time during the past 30 years! This generation of China's youth will not remain silent, they will not give up, they will not surrender! In the face of violence, let there be no doubt that we shall grit our teeth and join hands, unite once more, and for the sake of our nation and our motherland, for the sake of truth and for the sake of the future we shall explore new roads, overthrow tyranny, and establish a new society.

May 10th, 1979

References

[1] An example of a provincial reassessment is Xu Jiadun's report to the Jiangsu Party Committee in February 1979, to be found in Jiefang ribao ('Liberation Daily') p. 1. And then the possibility of a revised history for the whole of the thirty years since the establishment of the PRC is to be found in Ye Jianying, 'Meeting in Celebration of the 30th Anniversary of the founding of the People's Republic of China', (29 September 1979) in *Beijing Review* No. 40, 5 October 1979, p. 11-12.

[2] Thomas P. Bernstein, *Up to the Mountains and Down to the Villages – the Transfer of Youth from Urban to Rural China,* (Yale University Press, 1977).

[3] For one account see, Anne McLaren, 'The Educated Youth Return: The Poster Campaign in Shanghai from November 1978 to March 1979', in *The Australian Journal of Chinese Affairs* No. 2, July 1979, p. 1.

CHAPTER SEVEN

Conclusions: Socialist Democracy and the Potential for Dissidence

Two policemen observe the Revolutionary Martyr's Memorial, April 5th 1979

F

The events described in this book and the poems presented all date from the period November 1978 to April 1979. For a while it seemed that the Democracy Movement could and would stagger on in a reduced form despite the arrests of Wei Jingsheng, Chen Lu, Ren Wanding et al., and the restriction of activities to the area around Democracy Wall. Some activists attempted to disassociate themselves from those arrested by admitting, as did the 'April 5th Forum' for example, that there were 'some elements' within the Democracy Movement who had gone too far, but that they (that is the 'April 5th Forum') and the Movement in general were not against the Communist Party, its leaders, or socialism. Others reacted by concentrating on 'cultural democracy' and the publication of literary publications rather than openly political activities. Indeed unofficial publications were still published, and through the summer there were periods when wall posters flourished once again on Democracy Wall. In particular, there were peaks of activity at Democracy Wall around the anniversary of May 4th, during June and July when the 2nd session of the 5th National People's Congress met, and in the weeks surrounding the anniversary of Mao Zedong's death on September 9th. Even 'Exploration', whose publication had ceased with the arrest of Wei Jingsheng, began to re-appear in early September 1979. However, for the most part it was a very different Democracy Movement to that which had existed before March 29th 1979. Mild as the earlier Democracy Movement had been (as the selection of poems in this book clearly shows,) what followed was extremely bland. Perhaps the best example of that later phase of the Democracy Movement was the continued and regular publication of 'Truth' (*Qiushibao*). Anodyne to the point of embarrassment it appeared every fortnight, and not only presented material which was deliberately unprovocative but also to a large extent re-wrote articles which had recently appeared in the official press.

However, the Democracy Movement which had started with so much hope and optimism as an unregulated (i.e. by higher levels), spontaneous movement of expression, debate and questioning was well and truly buried in October and November 1979 with the trial of Wei Jingsheng[1] and the closure of the Xidan Democracy Wall.[2] Wei, the former editor of 'Exploration' was found guilty of being a 'counter-revolutionary', jailed for fifteen years and deprived of his rights as a citizen for eighteen. As of 8th December 1979, wall-posters can no longer be displayed at Xidan, but only on a newly designated wall at Yuetan Park (The Park of the Altar of the Moon), further west and less central. Furthermore even at Yuetan Park, poster writers have to register with the local police and provide details of their real name (if a pseudonym has been used), address, age and occupation. The specific characteristics of the Democracy Movement as a movement of protest in the People's Republic of China had thus all but disappeared by the end of 1979.

By its actions since the end of March 1979 the CCP has taken the first steps in attempting to draw a line between what is and what is not politically permissible in the new era of 'reconstruction'. In so defining its own 'Socialist Democracy', the party has thus run the risk of transforming what had previously been a movement of mild protest and dissent, and largely regime-supporting at that, into one of genuine dissidence and outright opposition. It is of course too soon to say whether in retrospect this will appear an inevitable consequence. Moreover, there certainly is more than one possible future given the doubts about both the popularity of the Democracy Movement and the leadership's official attitude.

The Democracy Movement was certainly popular in the sense that it was both of the people and on the streets. Its activities were often attended by large crowds and its unofficial publications invariably sold quickly. Indeed, on occasion, such as the sale of 'The Spring of Peking' (Number Four) at Democracy Wall on April 5th, there were scenes far more reminiscent of the Eton Wall Game than even the most crowded Beijing bookshop. It would be difficult to judge how much support each publication generated, although most regular publications had lengthy subscription lists in addition to street sales. Certainly, one cannot help feel that the Democracy Movement had a narrow social base, the 'under-privileged privileged' as previously suggested, which it either did little, or was unable, to expand. To write and publish a poem in the Democracy Movement, any poem, be it about petitioners dying in the cold or love for one's dead sister, was a political act. But it was a political act not just because of the role of poetry in the Tiananmen Incident of 1976, or because of the persecution of art and literature during the Cultural Revolution, but because it was an expressivist act. Yet, on the other hand, it should not be forgotten that China's age distribution is weighted heavily to those born since 1949, and the Democracy Movement may well have a future historiography of even greater popularity.

The regime's attitude to the Democracy Movement has not only fluctuated from the (apparently) extremely tolerant in November 1978, to the exact opposite a year later, but it has also always been ambivalent. Even now, when unofficial publications have been under attack, some works which were first published there, such as Zhang Yang's 'The Second Handshake', receive official praise and publication.[3] The situation thus remains ambiguous – there can be, and are, similar activities to before, only the rules are liable to change *ex post facto*. The regime's ambivalence seems even stranger if one considers that in a period when, as one is told, a new socialist legality is about to emerge[4] Wei Jingsheng should be given what amounts to a 'show trial'. He may very well be guilty, but justice has also to be seen to be done. One possible, although extremely cynical explanation, would be to suggest that Deng Xiaoping seemed to encourage the Democracy Movement at one time in order to prove a point to his colleagues, and then later no longer needed that particular headache. Such an explanation will undoubtedly be held by many. There is, however, another, more simple explanation to the paradox. As with the post-Stalin 'liberalization' in the USSR, the regime wants to encourage debate and dissent, but only loyal dissent and then only that under its control and within certain limits. The contradiction is thus that the leadership wishes to change the value system but that it has to rely on the old value system as the medium for change.

THE RIGHTS OF MAN
Ling Bing

This is an age-old tale
That has circulated for thousands of years.
Like so many beautiful stories,
One generation has passed it on to the next.
As an infant's wailing starts to rise,
A mother softly says: 'Child,
I wish you well!
You ought to be happy.
Life is equal and free.'
Yes, 'Life is equal and free,'
She is like the wind, like a spark,
Like a mighty tempest,
Reverberating in nature, in the universe,
For a long, long time.
The low murmur of the clock accompanies her,
Entering every humble thatched-roof shack.
This is an ancient dream.
The wind stealing across her face,
Constantly makes new wrinkles.
Nature has created you,
A dream who often sheds her own tears.

The primeval forest enveloping
Your first shrill call,
The pyramid's heavy work song,
The sound of clashing swords on the tournament field,
The crimson flame of the religious court,
A Fascist gangster's screaming bullet,
A sham-Marxist's frame-up.

Appearing briefly everywhere,
You collect humanity's every suffering.
Facing the hall of heaven you call out,

'Man – why – do you tyrannize man.'
Tyrants insult you,
Robbers scorn you,
Murderers hate you,
But, you are still you
– living, thriving you.

With your back facing the carried cross,
You proudly stand at the torch of the goddess of freedom!
From the first humiliation issuing forth from human hearts,
Humanity's descendants have been here with you,
Hobbling towards suffering.
The eyes of generations have been covered by darkness,
But you have represented them,
Humanity, burned to ashes,
To universal human barbarity
You have raised a new challenge!
You have lifted Spartacus's glistening sword,
You have proclaimed Galileo to humanity,
You have shattered the Bastille's prison gates,
You have liberated black slaves,
You have stood at the wall of the Paris Commune,
You have burst forth with:
'Workers of the world unite'.
You have waved the fluttering banner of 'April 5th',
You have followed 'April 5th' and stood
Amidst the tears of blood in Tiananmen,
You are the symbol of human strength and hope,
You are the suffering spirit's blazing bonfire.

I am a man,
I am all men.
I can proudly say
I have never failed you.
I believe, and so do you,
That one day
Humanity will be you,
And you
Will be humanity.

from *Science, Democracy and Law* No. 9, p. 8.

Notes

A major point of debate within the Democracy Movement and between the Democracy Movement and the Chinese Communist Party's leadership has concerned the concept of Human Rights. The Party has stressed the differences between socialist and capitalist democracy, the guarantee of rights in the constitution, and the need (to quote the *Beijing Daily* of 29th March 1979) for 'Not only democracy but also centralism, not only freedom but also discipline' and that the people's state implies both rights and obligations which can't be separated. Within the Democracy Movement there has been a wide range of attitudes to both democracy and human rights. The author's name is a pseudonym meaning 'Icicle'.

References

[1] For the official report of Wei Jingsheng's trial see NCNA (in English) 16 October 1979 and in SWB FE 6248/BII/1 18 October 1979.

[2] For the full text of Beijing Revolutionary Committee's new regulations governing democratic activities, see SWB FE 6293/BII/1 10 December 1979.

[3] First published in 'The Spring of Peking' Nos 1 and 2. See for example, Gu Zhicheng ' "The Second Handshake" a New Bestseller', in *Chinese Literature* No. 1. 1980, p. 101.

[4] See Peng Zhen's comments at the 2nd Session of the 5th National People's Congress in *Beijing Review* No. 28, op. cit.

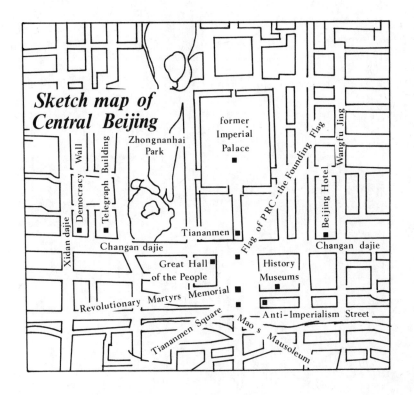

Sketch map of Central Beijing

Return to Tiananmen Square, p.41

再返天安门广场重祭
（一九七六年十月）

曾几何时洒祭觞，
而今擎旗返广场．
血染碑基花犹在，
扬眉怒看谁敢挡?!

肃立追思哀不尽，
弹泪浑归顾未偿。
天若有情天亦老，
漫天大雪落松墙。

APPENDIX 1

Original Editorials and Publication
Statements from Selected Unofficial
Publications

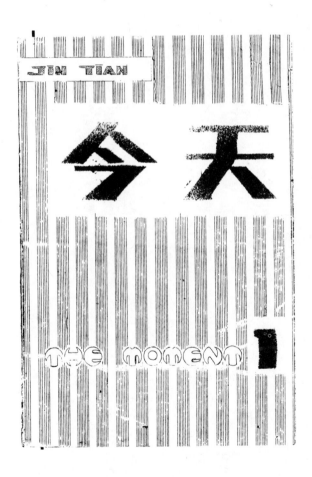

'APRIL 5th'

First number

Published by *April 5th Study Group*
28 November 1978

Advance Publication 26th November 1978

Aims:

To support the CCP
To support Chairman Hua as leader at the Party Centre
To study Marxism, Leninism, Mao Zedong Thought
To study the spirit of April 5th
To publish the people's thoughts and words, which for all kinds
   of reasons are not contained in official publications
To publish popular literature which develops the spirit of April
   5th
To work for the total transformation of modern Chinese society
To work for the realization of the four modernizations
To pay special attention to positive schemes, and not to be
   involved in negative ones
To promote unity and oppose divisions

'ANNOUNCEMENT OF PUBLICATION'

from *'Exploration'* No. 1. December 1978.

In order that the Chinese people's material and spiritual lives can reach the levels of the developed world, and that the social environment be as rational as possible given the basis of fast modernization, those comrades who have participated in the production of this publication pledge themselves to observe the following:

1. The freedoms of speech, press and assembly as provided in the Constitution shall be this publication's guiding principle.

2. This publication's explorations must be based on the realities of Chinese and world history. We do not accept that any one theory of any single person can be absolutely correct. All theories – and that includes those which exist at present and those which may soon emerge – can be discussed in this publication, as well as all techniques of analysis.

3. As the spokespeople of those who suffer, and taking the search for the cause of China's social backwardness as our main aim, this publication maintains that only the majority of the population, who are powerless and poor can define its cause and find a solution. This publication hopes in such a way to reach for the truth.

4. This publication plans to devote space to free discussion of social problems and only rejects vulgar and abusive language. It has matured in the factional and bureaucratic politics of the Cultural Revolution, and by opposing dictatorship at Xidan's 'Democracy Wall'. It opposes any opinion or theory which defends bureaucracy and dictatorial fascism. No one who does not give, and intends to refuse, freedom to others can use this publication.

5. This publication is prepared to receive articles and letters dealing with any problems within the framework of the principles above. This publication relies mainly on voluntary contributions. All contributions, articles, letters, printing paper, printing ink, and money can be sent to our editorial department in the same way this publication is received.

'PUBLICATION STATEMENT'
from '*The Spring of Peking*' No. 1. 8 January 1979, p. 1-2.

Many people predicted that when the China giant stood up it would shake the world. In 1949 it stood up but during thirty long years it has not exerted a commensurate gigantic influence. It has not only failed to surpass the imperialist powers, but has staggered along behind everyone else, dithering and hesitant. The people have eventually discovered that this once great nation has been wearing two shoes that were too tight – ignorance and tyranny. As a result China has failed to keep pace with the times, and cannot stand in the front ranks of the world's nations. Can it be that the Chinese people really lack the ability to do so?

For China to become rich and powerful, a socialist modernized power must be established – this has been the ideal long dreamt of by the Chinese people. But in order to take giant strides towards this great ideal, it is necessary to destroy modern feudalism and modern superstition, and gradually develop the two paths of socialist democracy and modern science.

This publication takes Marxism-Leninism as its guide, supports the Chinese Communist Party, adheres to the socialist road, and implements Comrade Mao Zedong's policy of 'Let a hundred flowers bloom, let a hundred schools of thought contend'. This publication is a comprehensive mass publication, which fully exercises the democratic rights of speech and publication as provided in the constitution, and will present the voices of the people and all kinds of exploratory articles.

The road ahead is hard and tortuous, but the people's desire for democracy and the state's for wealth and power are historical, irresistible trends. The fresh flowers of socialist democracy and science will brave blizzards and spring's chills to bloom proudly. Cleansed by the flames of the great and glorious 'April 5th' Movement, the Chinese people, with an indefatigable fighting spirit, greet 'The Spring of Peking' as a hundred flowers' bloom.

Notes

This is the original version of the 'Publication Statement', published in the very first edition. When reprinted in official magazine format (although without official backing) on 5th March 1979, the second paragraph was omitted and emphasis on party leadership added.

'TO OUR READERS'
The Editorial Board of '*Today*'[1]

At last history has given us the opportunity. Now our generation can sing the song that's been in our hearts for ten long years without bringing the sky down around our heads for a second time. We can't wait again, for to wait is to retreat, because history has already moved on.

As Marx points out:

> 'You admire the delightful variety, the inexhaustible riches of nature. You do not demand that the rose should smell like the violet, but must the greatest riches of all, the spirit, exist in only *one* variety? I am humorous, but the law bids me write seriously. I am audacious, but the law commands that my style be modest. *Grey, all grey*, is the sole, the rightful colour of freedom. Every drop of dew on which the sun shines glistens with an inexhaustible play of colours, but the spiritual sun, however many the persons and whatever the objects in which it is refracted, must produce only the *official colour*! The most essential form of the spirit is *cheerfulness, light*, but you make *shadow* the sole manifestation of the spirit; it must be clothed only in black, yet among flowers there are no black ones.'[2]

The Gang of Four's cultural despotism only allowed one kind of spirit, which was of a false form; they only allowed one kind of flower in the cultural forum and that was a black one. But '*Today*' produced with blood and tears is the dawn of today. What we need are multi-coloured flowers. What we need are flowers which really are from the world of nature. What we need are the unfettered flowers from the depths of people's hearts.

In the past, an older generation of writers added their blood and wrote more than a few magnificent works of literature. Our country's cultural history since 'May 4th' has been founded on these achievements. But now, speaking of them as a generation, they have fallen behind, and the tremendous and difficult task of reflecting the spirit of the new era has already fallen on our generation's shoulders.

'The April 5th' Movement marks the start of a new era. This new era must give everyone a purpose in life, and moreover go a step further in deepening people's understanding of the spirit of freedom; our country with its ancient civilization is taking on a new look, and must re-establish the position of the Chinese nation among the nations of the world. Our art and literature will then of necessity reflect its profound quality.

Today, as people open their eyes anew, we should never again take such a narrow view of 9,000 years of cultural heritage, but start to use a broader perspective to survey the surrounding horizons. Only in this way can we really discover our own value, and thereby avoid ridiculous conceit or deplorable self-defeat.

Our Today is rooted in the ancient fertile land of the past and in the belief that we would live and die for it. The past has already gone. The future is still far away. For our generation there is Today, only Today!

Notes

1 In its first issue *Jintian*, the title of the magazine in Chinese, was translated by the editorial board and appeared on the front cover as 'The Moment'. (See illustration p. 157.) In the second and subsequent issues *Jintian* appeared as 'Today'.
2 This quote from Marx carries no reference in the Chinese text of the editorial, although it does appear in quotation marks. It is from Marx's 'Comments on the latest Prussian Censorship Instruction', written in 1842 but not published until a year later, in Marx and Engels (*Collected Works*) Vol. I (Lawrence & Wishart, London, 1975), p. 112.

APPENDIX 2:

Checklist of Beijing Unofficial Press
November 1978–4 May 1979

BEIJING'S UNOFFICIAL PRESS
November 1978 – 4 May 1979

Name	*No.*	*Date*
Ban shen bu sui xixunbao ('Paralysis Good News')		
	1	February 1979
Beijing zhi chun ('The Spring of Peking')		
	1	8 January 1979
	2	27 January 1979
	3	17 February 1979
	1 (Selections from 1 and 2, printed)	
		5 March 1979
	4	5 April 1979
Huohua ('The Spark')	1	20 March 1979
Jiedong ('Thaw')		
	unnumbered	March 1979
	also dated Guiyang 27 February	
	1	24 November 1978
		originally published as
		Qimeng (Guiyang) No. 2
	2	March 1979
		originally published as
		Qimeng (Guiyang) No. 3
	3	March 1979
Jintian ('Today')		
	1	January 1979
	2	February 1979
	3	April 1979
		(Special poetry edition)
Kexue minzhu fazhi ('Science, Democracy and Law')		
	1	8 January 1979
	2	30 January 1979
	3	15 February 1979
	4	5 March 1979
	5	15 March 1979
	6	5 April 1979
	7	10 April 1979
	8	18 April 1979
	9	25 April 1979
	10	1 May 1979

Minzhuqiang ('Democracy Wall')

mid-December 1978

Minzhu yu shidai ('Democracy and the Era')

1	March 1979

Pugongying ('Dandelion')

1	January 1979
2	February 1979
3	March 1979
4	April 1979

Qimeng, Beijing ('Englightenment', Beijing Branch)

1	29 January 1979
2	24 March 1979

Qimeng, Guiyang ('Enlightenment', Guiyang Branch in Beijing)

1	11 October 1978
	reprinted Beijing 16 March 1979
2	24 November 1978
	claimed as *Jiedong* No. 1
3	8 January 1979
	claimed as *Jiedong* No. 2
4	25 March 1979
5	19 February 1979

Originally issues Nos 1 – 3 were produced in Guiyang and transported to Beijing. Numbering refers to the posters first displayed in Guiyang and then later in Beijing, which are in fact the contents of these publications.

Qimeng she bao ('Enlightenment Society News')

1	March 1979
2	April 1979

Qiushi ('Harvest')

1	20 March 1979
1*	March 1979
2	April 1979
2*	20 April 1979

Confusingly, the publishers of 'Harvest' produced two different editions of each issue. Those indicated here by * were not sold, like most of the unofficial press at Democracy Wall, and are identifiable by a red maple leaf on the cover.

Qiushibao ('Truth')

1	1 January 1979
2	1 February 1979
3	12 February 1979
4	1 March 1979
5	16 March 1979
6	11 April 1979

Quanmin gequ ('The All-people's Songbook')

1	3 April 1979
2	15 April 1979
3	29 April 1979

Qunzhong cankao xiaoxi ('Masses' Reference News')

1	23 December 1978
2	8 January 1979
3	3 February 1979
4	24 February 1979
5	24 March 1979
6	5 April 1979

Renmin luntan ('The People's Forum')

c.20 January 1979

Rexue ('Righteous Indignation')

1	1 May 1979

Shenghuo ('Live')

1	29 April 1979

Siwu luntan ('April 5th Forum')

1	16 December 1978
2	30 December 1978
3	6 January 1979
4	22 January 1979
5	10 February 1979
6	25 February 1979
7	11 March 1979
8	April 1979
9	May 1979

Siwu yuekan ('April 5th Monthly')

1	March 1979

Suishi ('Flint')

1	January 1979

Tansuo ('Exploration')

1	December 1978
2	29 January 1979
3	11 March 1979
Extra	24 March 1979

Wotu ('Fertile Land')

1	11 February 1979
2	8 March 1979
Special	2 April 1979

Xin tiandi ('New World')

1	March 1979

Yuanshangcao ('Grass on the Plain')

1	1 March 1979
2	30 March 1979

Zhongguo renquan ('China's Human Rights')

1	February 1979
2	March 1979
2*	22 March 1979
3*	5 April 1979
Special Edition*	7 April 1979

China's Human Rights Alliance split in March *inter alia* over China's war with Vietnam.

The editions marked with an * were published by the pro-War faction.

This checklist of Beijing's Unofficial Press makes no claim to be either comprehensive or exclusive. It is merely a compilation of all the unofficial newspapers and magazines known to have been circulating in Beijing between December 1978 and May 1979.

APPENDIX 3:

Glossary of Chinese Names, Terms and Places

The Administrative Office,
   of Zhongnanhai (qv) the headquarters of the party and
   government, and home of all China's top leaders. Until early 1979
   headed by Wang Dongxing (qv).

The Afang Palace
   built by Qin Shihuang (qv) the unifier of China (221 BC) near
   contemporary Xian. Destroyed by Chu Bawang at the end of the
   dynasty.

April 5th
   the date of the Tiananmen Incident in 1976, when there were
   demonstrations in Beijing's main square to the memory of Zhou
   Enlai and his policies and against those who have since become
   known as the 'Gang of Four' (qv) and their policies. The
   demonstrations which had been continuing for a few days before-
   hand, were finally broken up by the security forces on the evening
   of April 5th. At the time the Incident was labelled 'Counter-
   revolutionary' and led almost immediately to the dismissal of
   Deng Xiaoping. April 5th had thus become a symbol of resistance
   to the Gang of Four and the concepts of Cultural Revolution.
   Until late 1978 such activities were referred to unofficially as the
   'April 5th Movement' (or '4.5 Movement' in Chinese), making a
   parallel with the 'May 4th Movement' (qv) (5.4 Movement in
   Chinese) which started in 1919 with demonstrations in
   Tiananmen Square. However, in mid-November 1978 the Beijing
   Party Committee reversed the previous verdict on April 5th and
   now described it as 'a completely revolutionary event'.
   Subsequently, the term 'April 5th Movement' has been coined
   officially.

Baobashan
   the official cemetery for China's leaders.

The Big Five Red Guards
   the leaders of the Red Guard movement in Beijing during the
   Cultural Revolution. The five were:
   Nie Yuanzi from Beijing University
   Tan Houlan from Beijing Normal College
   Kuai Dafu from Qinghua University
   Han Aijing from Beijing Aviation Institute
   Wang Dabin from the Geological Institute.

The Chairman
always refers to Chairman Mao.

Changan Street
or the Avenue of Eternal Peace. Beijing's main thoroughfare, passing Tiananmen, Zhongnanhai and Democracy Wall (see sketch map). It is lined with trees.

Chen Yi
veteran army commander before Liberation and party leader. He was the first Mayor of Shanghai under the PRC and later Foreign Minister.

Democracy Wall
in fact two sections of wall, about 2.5 metres high and approximately 140 metres and 85 metres long, on the north side of Changan Street, next to the Telegraph Building and close by the Crossroads with Xidan Street (see sketch map). Wall-posters have regularly been posted there since 1977. From March 29th to December 8th, 1979 the display of wall-posters and holding of political meetings in Beijing has been confined to this wall and the area around it. When the Democracy Movement first started at the end of November, the wall and the area immediately around it was popularly referred to as 'Hyde Park' (after Speakers' Corner in London). However, since it has been popularly referred to as 'Democracy Wall'.

Deng Xiaoping
currently Vice chairman of the Chinese Communist Party, and Vice premier of the State Council. Popularly regarded as Zhou Enlai's successor. General secretary of the CCP before 1966, he was removed from office as a capitalist roader during the Great Proletarian Cultural Revolution. Rehabilitated in 1973, he was removed from office again in 1976 following the Tiananmen Incident. His second rehabilitation followed in the summer of 1977.

The Duke of Zhou
the minister of Wu Wang, the first emperor of the Zhou dynasty (11th century BC). Traditionally regarded as the model of a good administrator.

The Founding Flag
of the PRC, stands in Tiananmen Square opposite Tiananmen itself on the south side of Changan Street (see sketch map).

The Four Modernizations
of industry, agriculture, science and technology, and national defence. A policy originally associated with Zhou Enlai designed to modernize China by the end of the century and a guiding principle of national policy since 1976.

The Four Pests
originally a slogan of the Great Leap Forward referring to flies, rats, mosquitoes and sparrows which were to be destroyed. More recently used to refer to the 'Gang of Four' (qv).

The Gang of Four
Jiang Qing, Zhang Chunqiao, Yao Wenyuan, and Wang Hongwen. Four Politburo members who had risen to prominence during the Great Proletarian Cultural Revolution, and who were removed from office in October 1976 following Mao's death the previous month accused of having plotted a *coup d'état*.

The Golden Hoop
see The Monkey King.

The Hall of Great Harmony
the main audience chamber of the Imperial Palace in the Forbidden City in Beijing. It was where the Emperor conducted important business and so symbolized the Chinese Empire.

Ho Long
A veteran army commander, implicated in the removal of Peng Dehuai (qv), who died during the Cultural Revolution.

Hua Guofeng
Mao's successor as Chairman of the Chinese Communist Party; also Premier.

Jiang Qing
Mao's widow and one of the 'Gang of Four' (qv).

Jinggangshan
the first rural soviet of the CCP, organized by Mao Zedong and Zhu De after the failure of the party's urban strategy in 1929. Located on the borders of Hunan and Jiangxi, it was abandoned in 1934 when the Long March began.

Kang Sheng
although dead, a major target for the Democracy Movement. He had been a Politburo member, Adviser to the Cultural Revolution Group during the Great Proletarian Cultural Revolution, and was reported to have been involved in security work.

Li Dazhao
a major figure of the May Fourth Movement and one of the founders of the Chinese Communist Party. During the May Fourth Movement he was an editor of 'New Youth', a magazine produced by progressives at Beijing University.

Lin Biao
Minister of National Defence from 1959 to 1971, he became Mao's chosen successor during the Cultural Revolution. He is reported to have died in an air crash whilst fleeing to the USSR after having attempted an abortive *coup d'état*.

Lin Hujia
currently Mayor of Beijing and previously Mayor of Tianjin. He succeeded Wu De in the autumn of 1978.

Liu Shaoqi
the Number One Capitalist Roader during the Great Proletarian Cultural Revolution. Despite repeated suggestions of his posthumous rehabilitation this has not so far occurred, although his wife, Wang Guangmei, has received much publicity since January 1979. (Rehabilitated 1980.)

The May 4th Movement
is the name given in retrospect to the process of intellectual change in China from about 1915 to the early 1920s and embracing what was contemporarily referred to as the New Thought Movement, the New Culture Movement, and the New Literature Movement. The predominant themes of this process were the attempts to resist the encroachment of the Imperialist powers through national intellectual and institutional regeneration, based on a rejection of traditional values and the greater acceptance of Western ideas. The title of the movement refers to the day in 1919 when students from Beijing University demonstrated in Tiananmen Square against foreign domination

of China as symbolized by the Versailles Treaty which had just donated Shandong Province, previously a German colony, to Japan instead of returning it to China. Peaceful at first, the demonstration became violent when the students invaded the home of one of the Chinese officials whom they accused of having been responsible for agreeing to the transfer of Shandong. Arrests followed as did nationwide demonstrations demanding the release of those arrested, that the government should refuse to sign the Versailles Treaty, and the dismissal of the pro-Japan Chinese officials who had agreed to the Shandong transfer. Although the incident did not create the movement it did stimulate further the cultural and intellectual ferment that was already under way.

The Monkey King
a mischievous folk-hero with the ability always to come out on top whatever the adversity. According to legend, the gods in heaven became so annoyed with Monkey that weary of throwing him out they decided to control him. Ru Lai Wofo conquered Monkey and subdued him with a Golden Hoop. This hoop was placed round Monkey's head and if he started to do anything he shouldn't then it tightened and gave Monkey a headache. Under such control Monkey became the apostle of Tang Song, a monk, on a journey to the west. The mission completed, after many famous adventures, Monkey was given his freedom again as a reward.

Mount Tai
traditionally one of China's sacred mountains, regarded as the most important in the world. Situated in Shandong province it was a place to which many emperors came on pilgrimage.

New Youth
see Li Dazhao

Neva
the river on which Leningrad is sited. In 1918, Li Dazhao (qv) wrote openly welcoming the Bolshevik revolution.

Peng Dehuai
a veteran army commander and party leader. Minister of National Defence before 1959 when he clashed with Mao Zedong over the handling of the Great Leap Forward and was removed

G

from office. Although partially rehabilitated in 1962, he was criticized again during the Great Proletarian Cultural Revolution.

Peng Zhen
the Mayor of Beijing before the Cultural Revolution, he was its first major victim. Rehabilitated in January 1979, he is Chairman of the National People's Congress Legal Committee.

The Premier
always refers to Zhou Enlai.

Quin Shihuang
the unifier of China (221 BC).

Qing Ming
the Festival for Sweeping Graves is traditionally the time for remembering the dead. In 1976, it was the occasion for demonstrations in Tiananmen Square which led to the April 5th (qv) Incident. Demonstrators came armed with wreaths, garlands and poetry to Zhou Enlai's memory.

The Red Flag limousine
is China's largest and most luxurious home-produced automobile.

The Red Pavillion
was the name given to the Library at Beijing University during the May Fourth Movement. It was painted red and the first formal Marxist study group in China met there.

The Revolutionary Martyr's Memorial
stands in the middle of Tiananmen Square (see sketch map), and was erected to the memory of all those who fell before Liberation.

Shaoshan
Mao's birthplace in Hunan.

Sun Yat-sen (Sun Zhongshan)
founder of the anti-Manchu Tong Meng Hui and later of the Guomindang, Sun was one of the major leaders of the 1911 Revolution. Although absent at the time he was offered the presidency of the new Chinese Republic which he declined in favour of Yuan Shikai. He is regarded as the founder of the Chinese Republic.

Tao Zhu

former First Secretary of both Guangdong provincial CCP and the CCP Central Committee's Central-South Bureau before the Cultural Revolution. He became a Politburo member right at the start of the Cultural Revolution, but was removed from his official positions not long after. He was posthumously rehabilitated in December 1978.

The Three Do's and the Three Dont's

is one of Mao's exhortations which was first publicized shortly before Lin Piao's ouster in 1971: – practise Marxism, not revisionism; unite, don't split; be open and above board, and don't intrigue and conspire.

Tiananmen Square

the square in front of Tiananmen (The Gate of Heavenly Peace) in Beijing (see sketch map). It was formerly the gateway to the Forbidden City, and now serves as a reviewing stand for parades, mass meetings etc. ... It lies on the north side of the square. To the west is the Great Hall of the People, and to the east is the National History Museum. Mao's Mausoleum is to the south.

The Wall

always refers to Democracy Wall (qv) and not, as one might reasonably expect, the Great Wall.

Wang Dongxing

a major target of the Democracy Movement and Vice-chairman of the CCP. Long reputed to be in charge of the Administrative Office of Zhongnanhai (qv) the headquarters of the Politburo, State Council etc., and home of all China's top leaders. In Yanan, Wang is said to have been Mao's bodyguard, and ever since has been thought to have been involved in such security work. Since 1949, he has been at various times (amongst other things) a vice-minister of Public Security and Commander of People's Liberation Army Unit 8341, until early 1979 the Zhongnanhai guard, whose interventions in both the Tiananmen Incident of April 1976 and the arrest of the Gang of Four in October 1976 were important and publicized. In the first few months of 1979 he was rumoured to have become increasingly discredited and isolated – he was, for example, said to have ceased command of PLA Unit 8341 (which in turn had ceased to serve at Zhongnanhai) and to have conducted self-criticism.

Wang Hongwen
  one of the 'Gang of Four' (qv). Former Shanghai security cadre
  who became one of that city's leaders during the Cultural
  Revolution.

Wuchang
  one of the three former cities comprising present-day Wuhan, the
  provincial capital of Hubei, where the 1911 Revolution first
  broke out. Situated on the Yangtze river it is surrounded by hills,
  the tallest of which is Snake Mountain. The Red building is a
  block in the centre of town covered with slogans from the Cultural
  Revolution.

Xidan
  is the popular name for the area around the crossroads where
  Xidan Street (which runs north-south) meets Changan Street
  (which runs east-west). Democracy Wall is at Xidan (see sketch
  map).

Yao Wenyuan
  one of the 'Gang of Four' (qv). A journalist in Shanghai who
  became one of that city's leaders during the Cultural Revolution.

Ye Ting
  One of the leaders of the Nanchang Uprising in 1927, when the
  CCP attempted a strategy of urban revolution. Ding Si Bridge is
  in Nanchang.

The Yellow River
  one of China's two major rivers and the cradle of Chinese
  civilization.

Yuan Shikai
  the first president of the Chinese Republic after the 1911
  Revolution, who later usurped power and had himself crowned
  emperor.

Zhang Chungqiao
  one of the 'Gang of Four' (qv). A deputy secretary of Shanghai's
  party committee before the Cultural Revolution, who became the
  city's leading cadre in 1967.

Zhongnanhai
  the headquarters of the Politburo and State Council, and home

for China's top leaders. It is situated on Changan Street to the west of the former Forbidden City (see sketch map).

Abbreviations:

CCP	Chinese Communist Party
GPCR	Great Proleterian Cultural Revolution
NCNA	New China News Agency
PLA	People's Liberation Army
RMRB	*Renmin ribao* (People's Daily)
SWB FE	BBC summary of World Broadcasts, Part III, The Far East.

BIBLIOGRAPHY

A. *Primary Sources*
   1. **Serials**

Beijing Review
   – weekly. Formerly Peking Review.
Beijing Ribao (Beijing Daily)
Beijing Wenyi (Beijing Art and Literature)
   – monthly. Almost every provincial-level unit produces at least one literary or 'art and literature' magazine. Amongst the most daring and avant-garde during 1978/9 were *Shanghai Wenxue* (Shanghai Literature), *Sichuan Wenyi* (Sichuan Art and Literature) and *Anhui Wenyi* (Anhui Art and Literature).
BBC Summary of World Broadcasts, Part III, The Far East.
Chinese Literature
   – monthly, translations from official press. (Foreign Languages Press, Beijing.)
China Reconstructs
   – monthly.
The Daily Telegraph
   – only British newspaper with permanent representation in China. (London.)
Gongren Ribao (Workers' Daily)
Guangming Ribao (Illuminated Daily)
Jiefang ribao (Liberation Daily)
   – Shanghai Daily Newspaper.
Renmin Jiaoyu (People's Education)
   – monthly.
Renmin ribao (People's Daily)
Renmin Wenxue (People's Literature)
   – monthly.
Shehui Kexue Zhanxian (Social Science's Frontline)
   – quarterly published by Jilin People's Publishing House since May 1978.
Shi Kan (Poetry Monthly)
Shiyue (October)
   – quarterly literary magazine published in Beijing. First published August 1978.

U.S. Joint Publications Research Service, Translations on People's Republic of China
 – from National Technical Information Service, Springfield, Virginia, USA.
Xinhua yuekan
 – monthly digest of official press.
Zhongguo qingnian (China's Youth)
 – a monthly magazine which restarted in September 1978 after the Cultural Revolution.
Zhongguo qingnian bao (China's Youth News)

2. **Books, pamphlets, etc.**

Cong shiji chufa Xu Shijie
     (*Renmin chubanshe*, Shanghai, 1978)
Documents of the First Session of the Fifth National People's Congress of the People's Republic of China.
   (Foreign Languages Press, Peking, 1978.)
Geming shichao Tong Huaizhou (ed) (*Wenwu chubanshe*, Beijing 1977)
Geming shichao Editorial group of the 7th Ministry of Machine Building's Institute No. 502 and The Academy of Science's Institute of Automation. (*Zhongguo qingnian chubanshe*, Beijing, 1979)
Jianchi Makesizhuyi de Kexue taidu (*Renmin chubanshe*, Beijing, 1978)
Jianchi shehuizhuyi de minzhu yuanze Renmin chubanshe, Beijing, 1978)
Jianchi shishi quishi de geming zuoyong (*Renmin chubanshe*, Beijing, 1978)
Jianchi shishi qiushi de yuanze (*Renmin chubanshe*, Beijing, 1978)
Main Documents of the Second Session of the Fifth National People's Congress of the People's Republic of China.
   (Foreign Languages Press, Beijing, 1978.)
Ping Yao Wenyuan 'Ping xinbian lishiju "Hai Rui baguan"'
Su Shuangbi (*Renmin chubanshe*, Shanghai, 1979)
Renmin wansui (*Renmin chubanshe*, Beijing, 1978)
Shijian shi jianyan zhenli de weiyi biaozhun (*Hebei Renmin chubanshe*, Shijiazhuang, 1978)
Siwu yundong jishi Yan Jiaqi *et al.* (eds) (*Renmin chubanshe*, Beijing, 1979)
Tiananmen geming shiwenxuan
   Tong Huaizhou (ed) (no publisher, Beijing, 1978)

The Tiananmen Poems Edited and Translated by Xiao Lan
   (Foreign Languages Press, Beijing, 1979)
Tiananmen shichao Tong Huaizhou (ed) (*Renmin wenxue chubanshe,*
   Beijing, 1978)
Tiananmen shijian zhenxiang (*Renmin chubanshe,* Beijing, 1978)
Tiananmen shiwenji Tong Huaizhou (ed) of the Beijing No. 2
   Foreign Languages Institute. (*Beijing chubanshe,* 1979)
Yu wu sheng chu Zong Fuxian
   (*Shanghai wenyi chubanshe,* 1978)

3. Unofficial publications in translation

'Declaration of Chinese Human Rights'
   – in *Issues and Studies* (Taipei), Vol. XV, No. 11 (Nov. '79),
   p. 96.
'Declaration of *Chieh-Tung She* (The Thawing Society)'
   – in *Issues and Studies* (Taipei), Vol. XV, No. 11 (Nov. '79),
   p. 104.
'Democracy or the New Despotism'
   – by *Tansuo* (Exploration)
   Extracts in *Index on Censorship*, Vol. 8, No. 5, September-
   October 1979, p. 7.
'The Fifth Modernization: Democracy'
   – by Wei Jingsheng
   in *Documents on Communist Affairs 1980,*
   (Macmillan, London, 1980)
'The Fifth Modernization: Democracy'
   – by Wei Jingsheng
   Extract in *Index on Censorship*, Vol. 8, No. 5, September-
   October 1979, p. 9.
'On to the "Fifth Modernization" ',
   – by Wei Jingsheng
   in *Issues and Studies* (Taipei), Vol. XV, No. 11 (Nov. '79),
   p. 86.
Li Yizhe
'On Social Democracy and the Legal System'
   – in *Classified Chinese Documents: A Selection*
   (Institute of International Relations, Taipei, 1978),
   p. 350.
'Manifesto of the Alliance for Human Rights in China'
   – in *Index on Censorship*, Vol. 8, No. 5, September-October,
   1979, p. 3.

'Manifesto of the Enlightenment Society'
  – in *Issues and Studies* (Taipei), Vol. XV, No. 11 (Nov. '79),
  p. 102.
Political Program of the United Commission of the Hunan
Provincial Proletarian Revolutionists, (October 1967)
  – in *Classified Chinese Communist Documents: A Selection*
  (Institute of International Relations, Taipei, 1978), p. 269.
The Seventies
  – The Revolution is Dead Long Live the Revolution
  (Hong Kong, 1976)
United Commission of the Hunan Provincial Proletarian
Revolutionists
  – Whither China? (6 January 1968)
  in *Classified Chinese Communist Documents: A Selection*
  (Institute of International Relations, Taipei, 1978), p. 274.

B. *Secondary Sources*

Amnesty International Report *Political Imprisonment in the
  People's Republic of China* (Amnesty, London, 1978)
Bao Ruo-wang (Jean Pasqualini and Rudolph Chelnimski
  Prisoner of Mao (Penguin, Harmondsworth, 1976)
Barnstone, Willis (trans.) *The Poems of Mao Tse-tung* (Barrie &
  Jenkins, London, 1972)
Baum, R. (ed.) *China in Ferment* (Prentice-Hall, Englewood
  Cliffs, 1971)
Bennett, Gordon 'Traditional, Modern, and Revolutionary
  Values of New Social Groups in China' in Wilson, Wilson
  and Greenblatt (eds), *Value Change in Chinese Society*
  (Praeger, New York, 1979), p. 207.
Bergère, Marie Claire 'China's Urban Society after Mao' in
  Domes (ed) *Chinese Politics after Mao* (University College
  Cardiff Press, 1979), p. 155.
Bernstein, Thomas P. *Up to the Mountains and Down to the Villages*
  (Yale University Press, New Haven & London, 1977).
Bowden, Tom and Goodman, David S.G. *China: The Politics of
  Public Security* (Conflict Study No. 78, Institute for the Study
  of Conflict, London, 1976).
Bowden, Tom and Goodman, David S.G. 'The Heroes of Tien
  An Men' in Royal United Services Institute, *Journal for
  Defence Studies*, December 1976, p. 20.

Bowie and Fairbank (eds) *Communist China, 1955-59* (Harvard University Press, Cambridge Mass., 1965.)

Chan, Sylvia 'Political Assessment of Intellectuals before the Cultural Revolution' in *Asian Survey*, September 1978, Vol. 18, No. 9, p. 891.

Chang, Parris H. *Radicals and Radical Ideology in China's Cultural Revolution* (Research Institute on Communist Affairs School of International Affairs, Columbia University, New York, 1973).

Chen, Jack *Inside the Cultural Revolution* (Sheldon Press, London, 1976).

Chen Jo-hsi *The Execution of Mayor Yin, and other Stories from the Great Proletarian Cultural Revolution* (Allen & Unwin, London, 1979).

Chi Hsin *The Case of the Gang of Four* (Cosmos, Hong Kong, 1977).

Chi Hsin *Teng Hsiao-ping: a political biography* (Cosmos, Hong Kong, 1978).

Chou En-lai *In Quest* poems translated by Nancy T. Lin (Joint Publications, Hong Kong, 1979).

Chow Tse-tsung *The May Fourth Movement: Intellectual Revolution in Modern China* (Harvard University Press, 1960).

Churchward, L.G. *The Soviet Intelligentsia* (Routledge & Kegan Paul, London, 1973).

Cohen, Jerome A. *The Criminal Process in the People's Republic of China 1949-1953, An Introduction* (Harvard University Press, Cambridge Mass, 1968).

Cohen, Jerome A. 'The Criminal Process in China' in D. Treadgold (ed), *Soviet and Chinese Communism: Similarities and Differences* (University of Washington Press, London, 1967), p. 107.

Cohen, Jerome A. 'Due Process?' in Ross Terrill (ed) *The China Difference* (Harper & Row, New York & London, 1979), p. 237.

Dahl, Robert A. *Regimes and Oppositions* (Yale University Press, New Haven & London, 1973).

Djilas, Milovan *The New Class* (Allen & Unwin, London, 1957).

Domes, J. *China after the Cultural Revolution* (Christopher Hurst, London, 1977).

Eber, Irene 'Old Issues and New Directions in Cultural Activities since September 1976' in Domes (ed) *Chinese*

Politics after Mao (University College Cardiff Press, 1979), p. 203.

Esmein, Jean *The Chinese Cultural Revolution* (André Deutsch, London, 1975).

Gardner, J. and Idema, W. 'China's Educational Revolution' in Schram (ed) *Authority, Participation and Cultural Change in China* (Cambridge University Press, 1973), p. 257.

Goldman, Merle *Literary Dissent in Communist China* (Harvard University Press, 1967).

Goldman, Merle 'China's Anti-Confucius Campaign, 1973-74' in *The China Quarterly*, No. 63, p. 435.

Hinton, William, *Hundred Day War; the Cultural Revolution at Tsinghua University* (Monthly Review Press, New York & London, 1972).

Hong Yung Lee 'The Radical Students in Kwangtung during the Cultural Revolution' in *The China Quarterly*, No. 64, p. 645.

Hsia Chih-yen *The Coldest Winter in Peking* (W.H. Allen, London, 1978).

Hsu Kai-yu *The Chinese Literary Scene* (Penguin, Harmondsworth, 1976).

Huang Hsin-chyu *Poems of Lu Hsun* (Joint Publications, Hong Kong, 1979).

Index on Censorship Vol. 9, No. 1, February 1980. China since 1949.

Ionescu, Ghita *The Politics of the European Communist States* (Weidenfeld & Nicolson, London, 1967).

Ionescu, G. and de Madariaga, I. *Opposition* (Watts, London, 1968).

Kotewall, R. and Smith N.L. *The Penguin Book of Chinese Verse* (Penguin, Harmondsworth, 1962).

Kraus, R. 'Class Conflict and the Vocabulary of Social Analysis in China' in *The China Quarterly*, No. 69, p. 54.

Lane, David *The End of Inequality? Stratification under State Socialism* (Penguin, Harmondsworth, 1971).

Lane, David *Politics and Society in the USSR* (Weidenfeld & Nicolson, London, 1970).

Lapenna, Ivo *Soviet Penal Policy* (Bodley Head, London, 1968).

Leys, S. *The Chairman's New Clothes* (Alison & Busby, London, 1977).

Li, Victor 'The Rule of Law in Communist China' in *The China Quarterly*, No. 44, p. 66.

Li, Victor H. 'The Evolution and Development of the Chinese Legal System' in J. Lindbeck (ed) *China, Management of a Revolutionary Society* (George Allen & Unwin, London, 1972), p. 221.

Li, Victor 'Human Rights in a Chinese Context' in Ross Terrill (ed) *The China Difference* (Harper & Row, New York & London, 1979), p. 219.

Lifton, Robert J. *Thought Reform and the Psychology of Totalism* (Penguin, Harmondsworth, 1967).

Ling, Ken *Red Guard* (Macdonald, London, 1972).

Lu Hsun *Dawn Blossoms Plucked at Dusk* (Foreign Languages Press, Peking, 1976).

Lu Hsun *Wild Grass* (Foreign Languages Press, Peking, 1976).

Lu Hsun *Selected Works of Lu Xun*, Vol. III (Foreign Languages Press, Peking, 1959).

Lu Xinhua, Lu Xinwu, et al. *The Wounded: New Stories of the Cultural Revolution, 77-78* (Joint Publications, Hong Kong, 1979).

MacFarquahr, Roderick *The Hundred Flowers Campaign and the Chinese Intellectuals* (Praeger, New York, 1960).

Malden, W. 'A New Class Structure Emerging in China?' in *The China Quarterly*, No. 20, p. 83.

Mao Zedong *Selected Works*, Vols. I-V (Foreign Languages Press, Beijing).

Mao Tsetung *Poems* (Foreign Languages Press, Peking, 1976).

Medvedev, Zhores and Roy *A Question of Madness* (Penguin, Harmondsworth, 1974).

Montaperto, Ronald N. 'From Revolutionary Successors to Revolutionaries: Chinese Students in the Early Stages of the Cultural Revolution' in Robert A. Scalapino (ed) *Elites in the People's Republic of China* (University of Washington Press, Seattle & London, 1972).

Moody, Peter R. *Opposition and Dissent in Contemporary China* (Hoover Institution Publication 177, Stanford, 1977).

Nee, Victor *The Cultural Revolution at Peking University* (Monthly Review Press, New York & London, 1971).

Oksenberg, Michel 'The Institutionalization of the Chinese Communist Revolution: the Ladder of Success on the Eve of the Cultural Revolution' in *The China Quarterly*, No. 36, p. 61.

Reddaway, Peter 'The Development of Dissent and Opposition' in A. Brown and M. Kaser (eds) *The Soviet*

Union Since the Fall of Khrushchev (Macmillan, London, 1975), p. 121.

Rexroth, Kenneth *One Hundred Poems from the Chinese* (New Directions, New York, 1971).

Rothberg, Abraham *The Heirs of Stalin – Dissidence and The Soviet Regime, 1953-1970* (Cornell University Press, Ithaca & London, 1972).

Sakharov, Andrei D. *Sakharov Speaks* (Collins & Harvill Press, London, 1974).

Schram, Stuart (ed) *Mao Tse-tung Unrehearsed* (Penguin, Harmondsworth. 1974).

Schram, Stuart R. 'Introduction: The Cultural Revolution in Historical Perspective' in Schram (ed) *Authority, Participation and Cultural Change in China* (Cambridge University Press, 1973), p. 1.

Shirk, Susan L. ' "Going Against the Tide": Political Dissent in China' in *Survey*, Vol. 24, No. 1, p. 82.

Teng Hsiao-ping and the 'General Program' (Red Sun Publishers, San Francisco, 1977).

Terrill (ed) *The China Difference* (Harper & Row, New York & London, 1979).

Tökés, Rudolf L. *Opposition in Eastern Europe* (Macmillan, London, 1979).

Townsend, J. *Political Participation in Communist China* (University of California, Berkeley, 1967).

Vogel, Ezra F. 'Voluntarism and Social Control' in D. Treadgold (ed), *Soviet and Chinese Communism: Similarities and Differences* (University of Washington Press, London, 1967), p. 168.

Watson, Andrew J. 'A Revolution to Touch Men's Souls: the Family, Interpersonal Relations and Daily Life' in Schram (ed), *Authority, Participation and Cultural Change in China* (Cambridge University Press, 1973), p. 291.

White, Gordon *The Politics of Class and Class Origin: The Case of the Cultural Revolution* (Contemporary China Papers No. 9, Australian National University, 1976).

Whyte, Martin King 'Inequality and Stratification in China' in *The China Quarterly*, No. 64, p. 684.

Wilson, Wilson and Greenblatt *Deviance and Social Control in Chinese Society* (Praeger, New York, 1977).

Index of Poems by Unofficial Publication Title

INDEX OF POEMS BY UNOFFICIAL PUBLICATION TITLE

INDEX

民　意

——说点心里话

争　鸣

少有罪从何来，
奇冤何时说开。
无奈性已定下，
罪名冤沉大海。

德怀德高功重，
怀德有德华中。

冤情谁人知情？
枉事案情空洞。

贺老作战有功，
龙腾虎战夹勇。

功劳因何抹去，
高名内外轰动。

陈老总揽山岳，
教玉无瑕归白雪。
光明磊落著心胸，
荣中是豪杰。

陶铸因何遭难，
铸成栋梁肝胆。
何时名誉光复，
罪名何时削散。

彭真是好市长，
真才实能正当。

在京旧时多好，
哪时重归京堂。

如此沉冤莫白，
如此惨遭迫害。

如今大家有气，
如今大家来改。

同志朋友快来，
不亲从前无奈。

摆脱枷锁束缚，
向他们讨血债。

Frozen Land, p.98

冻土地

像白云一样飘过去送葬的人群，
河流缓慢地抱着太阳，
长长的水面被染得金黄。
多么寂静，
多么辽阔，
多么可怜的
那大片凋残的花朵。

Smoke from the White House, p.99

白房子的烟

白房子的烟
又细又长
那個女人慢慢地走向河滩……

那儿漂过去半段桅杆，
上面布满了破碎的弹片。

Song from the Little Wooden House, p.116

小 木 房 里 的 歌

——献给珊珊二十岁生日

为了你，
春天在歌唱。
草绿了，花红了，
小蜜蜂在酒浆里荡桨。

为了你，
白杨树弯到地上。
松鼠窜，杜鹃啼，
惊醒了密林中的大灰狼。

为了你，
乌云师了师垒廊。
雨珠落，水花飞，
洒在如痴的小河上。

为了你，
风鼓云帆去远航。
潮儿涌，波儿碎，
拍打着河边的小木房。

为了你，
小木房打开一扇窗。
长眠的哥哥醒来了，
睁开了眼睛向外望。

为了你，
小窗漏进一束光。
他蘸着心中的红墨水，
写下歪歪斜斜的字行

文革小组哪去了 ·怀德·

文革小组哪去了，　　纸船明烛照天烧。
牛鬼蛇神一网尽，　　玉宇澄清看今朝。

回想文革十年乱，　　难忘妖魔闹吃嚣，
康生老贼当顾问，　　组长"爬虫"江女妖。

下面一帮黑笔杆，　　枪杆坐阵是林彪。
党政军权一起夺，　　"五大领袖"跟着闹。

林彪闹事死得早，　　康生虽死民不饶，
王张江姚全逮捕，　　"五大领袖"随时敲。

搬起石头硬砸脚，　　一个一个全报销。
江山依旧红彤彤，　　一群苍蝇完蛋了。

*　　*　　*　　*　　*　　*　　*

愿尔恭学邓大人

——诗赠林乎加

一 速引天津水

烂々银河化雨霖，
谁知京畿竟无云。
愿君速引天津水，
勿负黎民久旱心。

二 恭学邓大人

长安父老待光临，
愿尔恭学邓大人。
剐骨疗毒除溃弊，
恩波下济拯纲伦。

三 必活百病身

日夜求医有泪痕，
忽逢起死一天神。
满腔信赖七个字，
妙手必活百病身。

四 花明柳岸春

亲躬艺圃育新林，
病树毒柯立断根。
再辨杂苗摇尾草，
自有花明柳岸春。

叼 赞林乎加

跃马横刀破铁柳，
弯弓再射暮天鸦。

风雷交响进军鼓，
敢压亡国后庭花。

走　　吧
——　给L

走吧，
落叶吹进深谷，
歌声却没有归宿。

走吧，
冰上的月光，
已从河床上溢出。

走吧，
眼睛望着同一块天空，
心敲击着暮色的鼓。

走吧，
我们没有失去记忆，
我们去寻找生命的湖。

走吧，
路呵路，
飘满红罂粟。